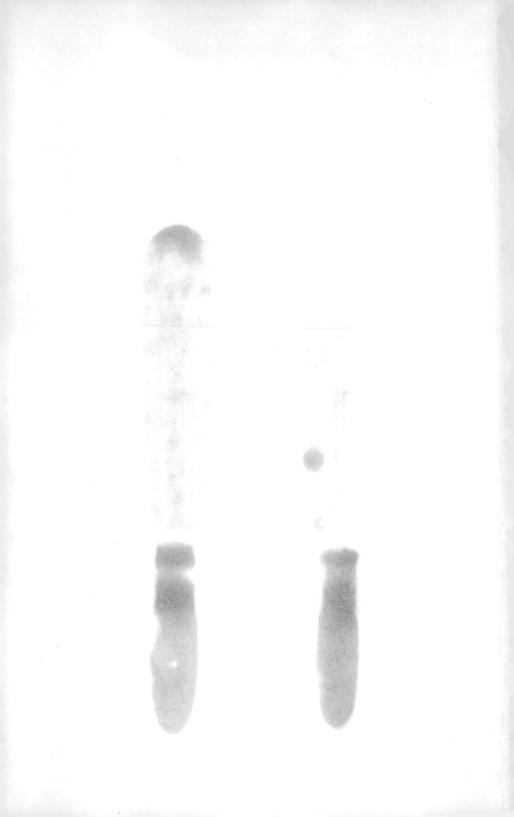

The Henry Morris Collection

The Henry Morris Collection

Editor

Harry Rée

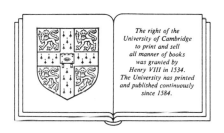

The right of the
University of Cambridge
to print and sell
all manner of books
was granted by
Henry VIII in 1534.
The University has printed
and published continuously
since 1584.

Cambridge University Press

Cambridge

London   New York   New Rochelle

Melbourne   Sydney

Published by the Press Syndicate of the University of Cambridge
The Pitt Building, Trumpington Street, Cambridge CB2 1RP
32 East 57th Street, New York, NY 10022, USA
296 Beaconsfield Parade, Middle Park, Melbourne 3206, Australia

© Cambridge University Press 1984

First published 1984

Printed in Great Britain by the University Press, Cambridge

Library of Congress catalogue card number: 84-45420

British Library Cataloguing in Publication Data

Morris, Henry
The Henry Morris Collection
1. Education
I. Title   II. Reé, Harry
370   LB775.M8

ISBN 0 521 26612 2

UP

Contents

Acknowledgements

We are grateful to the following for permission to reproduce articles
in this collection: Jarrolds of Norwich for 7 *Adult Education*; British
Broadcasting Corporation for 8 *The Village College*, 12 *Liberty and the
Individual and* 15 *The Idea of a Village College*; R.I.B.A. Journal for
14 *Architecture, Humanism and the Local Community*; County of
Cambridgeshire and Lionel Morris Sheldon for the rest.

We should also like to express our gratitude for help from the following:
Charles Beresford (Senior Inspector for Humanities and In-Service Education.
Cambridgeshire); Maurice Dybeck (Warden, Sawtry Village College, Cam-
bridgeshire); Brian Hicks (Community Education Officer, Cambridge);
Geoffrey Morris (Chief Education Officer, Cambridgeshire).

Cover photograph of Henry Morris reproduced courtesy of Jack Pritchard

Introduction

by Harry Rée

His life and times

Henry Morris was Chief Education Officer for Cambridgeshire from 1922 to 1954. In a period of successive financial cuts and crises, and with a county council which could never have been classified as a big spender, he transformed education in this small rural authority. Through the establishment of the village colleges he laid the foundations of a new and greatly extended system of education, now called community education. The system could not be contained for long within the boundaries of Cambridgeshire; already during Morris's lifetime, and even faster after his death, it spread to many other parts of the country and is still spreading.

Morris can be seen as a man of three centuries. Born in 1889, he retained throughout his life many of the admirable attributes of the Victorian reformer. In the present century he initiated single handed one of the great steps forward in education theory and practice. For the twenty-first century he was both a prophet and a builder. Many would claim that the huge social and economic problems of the future can be acceptably tackled only by the kind of radical changes in education and schooling which he foresaw and by the establishment of new institutions; these he began to build in Cambridgeshire. It was no passing whim which caused him to have printed on the front of a festival programme in 1931 these lines from Meredith's poem 'The Empty Purse'.

> Thou under stress of the strife
> Shalt hear for sustainment supreme
> The cry of the conscience of life:
> Keep the young generation in hail
> And bequeath them no tumbled house.

It is of course as a prophet and a builder that he lives on, and while the building of community schools and colleges goes ahead everywhere, it is important and useful to rescue from the moths and mice the words and ideas which were originally behind both these developments and many other reforms which he preached and promoted during his lifetime. And it is appropriate that Cambridge University Press should join in that rescue, since it was the University Press which he commissioned, in 1924, to print his memorandum, 'The Village

College'. This was the first of his published writings, in which he sketched out the plans that were to occupy him for the next thirty years. The *Memorandum*, as it has come to be called, (thus avoiding the sonorous and evocative nineteenth-century sub-title) is quite rightly placed first in this selection of his most important articles and speeches, not only for chronological reasons, but it is surely the most impressive and important. These 'relicts' form the bulk of the material that he left behind to express the ideas and ideals which moved him during his lifetime. They influenced and impressed many who read them or heard them at the time. They have the power still to influence and impress. In his writing he expressed himself (to use his own phrase) in 'athletic prose' and when speaking in public he would often employ a characteristic rhetoric. Jacquetta Hawkes has said of him: 'Addressing an audience Henry could look and speak like a prophet, with telling passion and authority. I have seen a large council of worldly and successful men so moved by his address on what our cities were like and what they might become, that for an hour or so they had faith that something could and must be done.'

But he never got around to writing a book. Quite simply this was because he was too busy. This may also explain and excuse certain faults in his articles and speeches. There are occasional obscurities, occasional misquotations, and here and there repetitions, not just of phrases but of whole paragraphs which he would lift from a previous speech or article. Such repetitions he no doubt included, partly because he was busy, but more likely because he had an important message to get across, and his articles and speeches, apart from the presence of the village colleges themselves, were the main means he had of conveying his message.

In these pieces will be found a deeply-rooted rational philosophy fed by an almost religious idealism. These two sources of strength, rationalism and idealism, informed his life as a constructive administrator and reforming educator. They caused him to become, during his lifetime, an important influence not so much on his colleagues or contemporaries, but among the young whom he befriended; in many of these he inspired lasting admiration and great affection. His circle of friends and disciples was not very large but they were loyal and many moved in later life to positions of power, particularly in the world of education. Here they have acknowledged his influence, often publicly, while they promoted in their own ways his ideas and plans for a massive extension of education in the broadest sense of the word.

Before starting this collection of his more incisive thoughts it is perhaps worth briefly recalling the man, his times, and his achievements. Henry Morris invented the community school; he created the village college. He introduced the New Architecture to school building and put colour and original works of art into schools and classrooms. He advocated the abolition of the 'insulated school'; he inveighed against passive learning and called for radical reform in the traditional curriculum, which he saw as inappropriate for all but a few; he was the first to put forward a workable scheme for lifelong education for all, and for the democratisation of education through extending control to the community.

He was shy, but he could seem eccentric, and even shocking, both in public and private. To many he was oddly enchanting but to the same people, often he could be maddening. Very generous at times, he could be mean and even occasionally petty. A homosexual, he was repelled by the effeminate and believed firmly in the family. An ex-elementary schoolboy and a convinced socialist, his lifestyle was aristocratic. Deeply moved by music, painting and poetry and fascinated by architecture, he welcomed a future controlled by science and by civilised planning. He inspired in his friends undetachable loyalty, but he made and kept a number of implacable enemies.

There was a gap between his private and his public life which he maintained with care, but there was a connection, indeed the one nourished and reflected the other. The flowers in his elegant flat in Trinity Street, his concern that his dining table should be properly furnished, whether with silver and china or with well-chosen food and wine, the near obsession with his physical health and his delight in natural beauty and with all the arts, all these personal concerns were carried over into his public and professional life. He went to great trouble to ensure that 'his' schools and the village colleges were designed, decorated and furnished with good taste, that school dinners should be served and eaten with decorum and some formality; he liked to see fresh flowers in schools but let it be known that they should never be stuck in jam jars! In making such connections he was only following a pattern common to all great teachers, who are moved to share what they love with those they teach.

Like a meteor he lit up the dark skies of the thirties. After the war he began to decline. By the end of his life he was burnt out. But his words and his works remain a force today.

He belonged to a generation, perhaps the last in English history, who were ashamed of their origins. He concealed even from close friends the fact that his father was a plumber in Southport and that he came from a large and respectable lower-middle class family. After leaving school at 14 he worked on a weekly paper, the *Southport Visitor*. He continued his education by attending adult classes in Preston and in 1910, at the age of 21, he was accepted at St David's College, Lampeter, to train for the priesthood. But here he felt confined and uneasy. After two years and a public row with the principal, he gained entry to Exeter College, Oxford.

He was deeply moved by Oxford, by the intellectual stimulation, by the architecture and the Cotswold countryside, and by his friendships. Many years later, after a brief visit there he wrote: 'Oxford looked magnificent; great and gracious city. I went round and saw my former rooms and thought of the golden hours there long ago, and all my dear friends killed in the war...'

By November 1914 he had joined up and was later commissioned in the Royal Army Service Corps. From 1915 to 1919 he served as a staff officer in Italy. For him, as for many young men who had not been to public schools, and who became officers during the war and survived, the experience was transforming. Not only did he learn how to take administrative responsibility but, more important, he learned how to exercise authority in accordance with the accepted English model. By the time he was demobilised he had adopted the gestures, carriage and tone of voice of the successful product of the English public school.

He still had one year to complete his degree. He chose to avoid Oxford with its poignant memories and was accepted at King's College, Cambridge, read philosophy and after four terms he was awarded an upper second. He had, by now, given up the idea of entering the Church and although he had abandoned his Christian beliefs he had by no means abandoned his attachment to the words of the Bible and Prayer Book. Nor did he turn his back on the importance for humanity of retaining opportunities for ceremonies and for meditation.

From Cambridge he moved to Kent where the Director of Education, E. Salter Davies, had established informally a school of 'assistants' whom he correctly saw as budding education officers. Morris was the first of a distinguished team to take on administrative responsibility for a county education authority. In 1921 he went as assistant to the Chief Education Officer of Cambridgeshire, but after a year, the chief suddenly dying, he replaced him. He was 33 years old.

The village college was the main instrument through which he would apply his ideas for what he called 'the extension of education', so that education would become a source of liberation and a means of grace for the whole adult and adolescent population, the extension going far beyond lessons in classrooms or courses in schools, extending into 'all those activities which go to make a full life: art, literature, music, festivals, local government, politics'.

In the summer of 1924, while staying with a friend in the Cotswolds, he composed his first plan for the future of rural education. Cambridgeshire would be a test bed for the scheme. He had it printed as a memorandum and sent it to every member of the county council. Rightly it has pride of place in the collection which follows. After the carefully expounded details of his plan we come to the rhetorical apostrophe addressed to the architect. It rings out like the exhortation of an Old Testament prophet.

The *Memorandum* was accepted gratefully by his committee, but they took three years to approve the scheme for the building of the first village college at Sawston, and it was three more years before the building was opened. When financial stringency and government cuts caused delays he set about raising money and even equipment from private sources and private firms in order to get Sawston completed. 'I gave my blood for Sawston,' he once said, 'my blood, not my sweat.'

But, even while striving for this one first exemplar, he was planning three more, and to this end, tired of doubting councillors and their lack of vision, he borrowed twenty pounds from his brothers and took a boat to America. He had a letter of introduction to the Spelman Foundation and he returned at the end of 1929 with a cheque for £45,000 which he proceeded to wave before his committee; it caused the chairman of the county finance committee to remark: 'We have got a real plum!'

The following three years were marked by the Wall Street Crash, and the Great Depression. One of the immediate echoes from this was a freeze on all new school building, which lasted till 1934. They were years of infuriating frustration. He described his irritations and his ways of escape in a letter to his friend Charles Fenn in 1932:

I have been living for two weeks in a world of administration, of regulations, of abstract curricula, of educationl 'isms' dry as dust; indeed, dusty as death; of reports, resolutions and recommendations discussed ad nauseam by dried up old men and women with bald heads and spectacles and all withered from the armpits downwards; a valley indeed of dry bones in which there is no life and no suspicion of beauty, truth and goodness. But above all no apprehension of light and delight, of impulse and passion; of Art at once sensuous and sensual; of the satisfaction of pure intelligence; of food and wine; of the imperious demands of the body; of love encounters, most vehement and prodigal...of sexual congress in which all reality seems to be absorbed and ultimately quieted, with calm of mind, all passion spent; or sunlight on the English countryside, morning sun in cornfields; the moon on the river; chicken and salad and claret cup for supper; dozing conversation in the Library...

That vehement outburst about his work should not be seen as an indicator that he was not an efficient and conscientious administrator, nor was his imaginative energy, whether expressed in his private or professional life, in any way dimmed or clouded by the demands of the education office. Norman Fisher, who became Chief Education Officer for Manchester, started as his assistant in Shire Hall and wrote of him: 'Only those who worked with him can appreciate the minute and thorough devotion to detail, the intense concentration he could bring to any administrative problem, however humdrum'.[1] His own attitude to administration is almost startlingly put in the broadcast, printed in full in this collection (page 109). 'Administration is only safe when it is in the hands of the philosopher and thinker, the teacher, the artist and the saint, for whom administration exists merely as the instrument for realising quality...'

After the ban on new building was lifted, progress was resumed almost frenetically. In other letters to the same friend mentioned earlier we can follow the process through:

May 1934
I've just got off an appeal to the Carnegie Trustees for £10,000 towards the cost of three more village colleges

November 1934
Fortunately we have decided to put up three more village colleges, and I'm engaged all my waking hours thinking out the architecture and equipment. I had Gropius, the German architect staying with me a few weeks ago...and his conversation and many months of study of modern architectural techniques, confirm me in the necessity of doing all contemporary buildings without regard to traditional style.

December 1934
I have just secured £3,000 from the Carnegie Trustees for parts of our three new village colleges which are to cost £50,000.

October 1936
I have had to cut my holiday short in view of the need to secure the [Impington] V.C. scheme. The building is to cost £30,000 and Gropius has

---

1 'Henry Morris. Pioneer of education in the countryside'. Arthur Mellows Memorial Lecture, 1965.

produced a wonderful plan which will be the most advanced rural community centre in this country. Meantime Bottisham Village College will be finished in January when it will be opened by the Education Minister, and Linton Village College will be finished in March. I shall feel then, with four V.C.'s the idea is permanently safe. I read a paper on the subject at the September meeting of the British Association at Blackpool (see page 48) and went off the deep end.

January 1937

I am in a sea of troubles with the Gropius scheme. He is shortly to go as Professor of Architecture to Harvard. So U.S.A. gets him. I think I shall finally pull off G's scheme, but it will be difficult.

December 1937

Linton and Bottisham Village Colleges are completed and working and Impington will start building in a month's time. The latter is a masterpiece.

February 1939

Gropius' building is almost finished and will be opened by Lord Baldwin (!) Chancellor to the University, in September next...It will I believe be the most distinguished modern building in Britain.

The sudden appearance of the German architect, Gropius in this country exerted a powerful influence on him. Until the thirties he had favoured classical and Georgian architecture; but he was gently and gradually converted to the Modern Movement by one of his oldest friends, Jack Pritchard, and by others. Soon he became conscious of the need to support contemporary artists, architects and craftsmen, not only for artistic reasons but on moral grounds, for we have a duty, he felt, to buy or commission works from artists who are alive. So when Pritchard first introduced him to Gropius, who was in effect the founder of the Modern Movement in Europe, the meeting was electric; the two men got on from the beginning. When Gropius came out of Germany, since his liberal ideas were not tolerated by Hitler, and it seemed that he might settle permanently in Britain, Morris enthusiastically pursued the idea of getting him, in conjunction with Maxwell Fry, a British architect of the New School, to design Impington Village College. The building which emerged from this meeting has been recognised as the originating influence behind the best designed schools of the post-war period. Pevsner, in *The Buildings of England*, Penguin (1954) described it as 'one of the best buildings of its date in England, if not the best'.

Lord Baldwin did not come and open Impington in September 1939 for obvious reasons, but the war, although it put a stop to school building and official openings, certainly did not stop Morris from active thinking, nor from disseminating his thoughts in articles and speeches. It is significant that five out of the fifteen items in this collection came out between 1941 and 1944. Like many people who were prevented, usually by age, from taking an active part in the war, this fallow period offered a welcome breathing space seriously to criticise the past and constructively to plan the future. The first object of his criticism was the traditional school, and in particular the traditional curriculum. In a paper quoted below (page 69) he wrote: 'Our state educational institutions, particularly the schools, are classroom-ridden, lesson-ridden, textbook-ridden, information-ridden and given over to incessant didactic discourse and discursiveness...'

And in another paper (page 86) he emphasised the vital importance of local government: 'We tend to forget,' he wrote, 'that local government is also a cornerstone of freedom as every dictator realizes when, on getting into power, he abolishes it (Napoleon in France, Mussolini in Italy, Hitler in Germany).' Surely we should not forget this warning whenever central government makes a move to extend its power.

After the war, while continuing to press (successfully) for additional village colleges to be opened in Cambridgeshire, he was offered, by the government, opportunities to exercise his imagination and talents in the wider world. Early in 1947 he visited West Africa at the invitation of the Colonial Office to advise on the future development of the West African Institute of Industries, Arts and Social Sciences, based in Accra. The fruits of the three-month visit were meagre: a much delayed report full of sensible suggestions which were never acted upon, and a typically acid remark he made in full council on his return. He stressed, for example, the need for trainee designers to be taught both by a craftsman/technician as well as by an artist/designer. (Echoes here of the Bauhaus.) He insisted too that architects and planners should be continually conscious of the social forces which would necessarily impinge on their plans and their buildings. (Would that post-war British architects had successfully noticed this point.) And there was a paragraph which must have struck the Colonial Office as somewhat irrelevant, where he spelt out the reason why the co-operative workshops in West Africa which he visited and admired, were a new and exciting example of adult education; 'Through them, education is connected with vocation and with the mastery of a particular skill, through which the man or woman makes a contribution to the community...Here is the instrument for a genuine adult education. At all levels man achieves status, both mentally and socially... It is in this context that adult education with a vital relevance can be carried on.'

Obviously he visited schools in the course of his travels and he was horrified at what Western education was doing to the spontaneous artistic expression still alive in African children: 'In Africa,' he wrote later,[1] 'you will see boys and girls capable of drawing beautifully even on their bodies and of dancing significantly. A term spent on reading and listening to discourse on books which turn poetry and literature into educational subjects, reinforced by a fortnight of arithmetic and a month of raffia, kills all this stone dead.'

A memorable remark which emerged from the visit came when a hostile councillor asked Mr Morris: 'Who does *your* work when you are away from the office so often?' 'Precisely the same people who do it when I am not away,' he replied.

A second opportunity came when, just before his visit to Africa, the county council was asked to release him for two days a week in order to advise the Minister of Town and Country Planning, Lewis Silkin, on the cultural and community aspects of the work of creating new towns. But he returned from his hot and exhausting two months in West Africa to a Cambridge swept by east winds and icy sleet. He fell ill with pneumonia. It was not until the summer of 1947 that he was able to start on his part-time job at the ministry. Like the African visit this new job bore fruit mainly in words and ideas (see page 113). The people he had to work with, civil servants and the officers of other local authorities, did not take to his style any more than to his suggestions. His ideal of a multi-dimensional complex which would cater for all ages and offer opportunities for both study and recreation was strong meat, for most officials it was indigestible.

So his influence was waning, and although his attachment to the ministry produced little, it did convince him, and indeed some others, that the village college need no longer be only a rural phenomenon, and that the urban community was as much in need of the 'extension of education' as the country town. In 1954 he retired completely from his Cambridgeshire office; he continued to work for the ministry, but he became ill from time to time and the work was frustrating.

One final act of imaginative construction occupied his last years. Exerting himself to get money and to assemble a committee of friends of the Arts, most of whom were friends of his, he established at Digswell Lodge near Welwyn Garden City, a community of artists

1 *Amusement and Education*, paper read to the All Souls Group, October 1953.

and craftsmen, providing each with a studio and a flat and as far as he could manage to do so, with a philosophy consonant with his own. It would be an open community, going out to the neighbourhood and welcoming to visitors; thus the artist would become, as he put it, as accepted by ordinary people as is the doctor or the teacher. Tenants were recruited; some were enthusiastic, others were critical, especially of Morris himself, who was aging fast, so that his memory and his health began to go. One of the tenants wrote:

At the beginning he was a very active man, cycling round the Garden Citry on his old Lady's bike with a little wicker basket on the front...His twinkling eyes and whimsical humour captivated us. But later the shuffling steps along the corridor leading to our studio, confirmed by the snuffling of a continually running nose, would cause us to pray for deliverance...

And yet, generously, another member of the group admitted later that they had been wrong about Morris. They had somehow got the idea that Digswell Lodge was backward looking, an attempt to set up the artist and craftsman in the William Morris mode, as someone special to be revered and protected. But he wrote later:

Digswell, far from looking back, heralds the future; the need for people everywhere to be involved directly in creation, and particularly in art, is now much more obvious...I now realise that Henry saw this very clearly before many others and worked in a tangible way to do something about it. Digswell was part of this.[1]

After his retirement he had been forced to move out of his Cambridge house – full of his household gods – his carefully collected furniture, pictures, silver. He lived for a while in London, but hated it. Finally he took two rooms in a hotel in the Garden City to be near to Digswell. Here he declined, lonely, even though visited by loyal friends. He died on 10 December 1961.

[1] The Digswell Project is described in *Educator Extraordinary. The life and achievement of Henry Morris* (pp. 116–124) by Harry Rée. Longman 1973.

1

The Village College

Introduction

The *Memorandum* must have seemed a remarkable document in 1924 when it dropped, with their Christmas mail, through the letter boxes of the county councillors of Cambridgeshire. Here was a local government servant, whom they had only recently promoted to being Secretary for Education, taking it upon himself to have printed at his own expense, a long-term plan for the development of education in the county. In it he explored the past, the present and the future. Nor did he confine himself to schools. He touched on agricultural economics, youth training, the social and political life of villages and at length on architecture. A later edition, reprinted early in 1925, was only slightly different. It included a striking quotation from the *Times Educational Supplement*, which was placed immediately after the title page. This usefully lent weight to Morris's argument. It reads:

'The rural problem is one that successive governments have ignored in despair. The elementary school buildings are inadequate and insanitary in an appalling proportion of cases; the lack of facilities for continued and secondary education is a disgrace to a highly organised community. All [the necessary] things can be done. What we wish to emphasise is the fact that in rural districts they are not being done, and do not seem likely to be done.'
13 December 1924

Among the bodies to which he sent the report were the Board of Education, the Ministry of Agriculture, the Carnegie Trustees, the Development Commissioners (who were responsible for recommending schemes for post-war reconstruction) and the National Council of Social Service. Lord Hadow's committee, which at the time was considering post-primary education, acknowledged the receipt of the *Memorandum*, saying that they 'would consider the scheme'. The rather curt reception was perhaps surprising since Morris's plan for Cambridgeshire, which involved separating the elementary schools into separate junior and senior schools was exactly what Hadow eventually proposed, two years later in his committee's report: *The Education of the Adolescent*.

The document remains remarkable 60 years later. Not only is it still readable, because well written, but much of it is still relevant to the problems we have to face today both in the countryside and in the towns. Like the sub-title, with its generous use of capital letters, the prose reflects the style of the Victorian essay. But the content looks forward with visionary courage, towards a realisable ideal.

The early paragraphs set the scene in a Cambridgeshire landscape, which has long since disappeared. Here the country lanes connecting farm and village had three tracks, not two, the middle one being trodden bare by the cart-horses. Crops were poor and in the fields, in summer, wheat and barley contended with poppies and cornflowers. The farms were lit at night by candles or oil lamps, and in the elementary schools children from the age of sometimes three to fourteen were contained often in only two classrooms.

Morris started by pointing out the need for administrative reform by which the older children in the elementary schools would be offered a separate and suitable school experience in senior schools. But this, he asserted, was not enough. 'If rural England is to have the education it needs and the social and recreational life it deserves, more is required than the reorganisation of the elementary school system, and that which is required is possible.' At this point he describes his plan for a network of village colleges, and explains how the various educational and social agencies, which at present offer their services separately, could be grouped together 'around one institution'. He shows clearly, not only his vision, but his almost meticulous attachment to detail, as for instance when he writes of the simple shower baths and dressing room which should be provided for the village athletes (item 9 of Paragraph X). Here, as elsewhere (for example in Paragraph XII), he betrays a surely half-conscious concern that the village colleges should offer the country people some taste of what Oxbridge offered their highly-privileged students.

Paragraph XIII presents readers today with a small problem because, although obviously written by Morris and existing in some versions of the *Memorandum*, it does not appear in them all. This collection presents the fuller version. This section stresses the opportunity for voluntary bodies to play an even more important part in local life if they could operate within the compass of the village college. Possibly Morris felt that this would appeal to his local councillors to whom he sent the original, but that the trusts and government agencies and departments to which he sent the later edition would be less interested in such issues.

The final paragraphs contain some of his most expressive and even lyrical writing, especially when he addresses the imagined architect of the college. In the penultimate paragraph he becomes again the meticulous administrator, putting forward a scheme for the establishment immediately of colleges in two specified villages. He brings the whole essay to a conclusion with the tempting suggestion that Cambridgeshire could become a 'demonstration area for rural reconstruction' making possible 'a really massive contribution to the rural problem which it could be said without exaggeration would surpass anything that has been done in any country.'

Cambridgeshire has, in fact been a demonstration area for the Morris vision of community education, but it is rather more a demonstration to the nation of what he prophetically wrote at the end of Paragraph XV: 'The village college would not outlive its function, for the main reason that it would not be committed irrevocably to any intellectual or social dogma... it might be one of the freest of our English institutions.'

The Village College

Being a Memorandum on the Provision of
Educational and Social Facilities for the Countryside,
with Special Reference to Cambridgeshire.

Printed at the University Press, Cambridge 1924.

Education and rural welfare

I The immense development of the state system of education in
England during the nineteenth and present centuries has been almost
wholly an urban development. The towns are rich, and as they are
centres of large populations the provision of schools and institutes for
higher education has not been administratively difficult because the
pupils live in hundreds and thousands at their very doors. The
elementary schools of the towns are, on the whole, better built and
more generously staffed and equipped than those of the countryside;
secondary schools, with a few exceptions, are situated in the towns;
so also are the centres of technical education. The most vigorous and
systematic popular movement for adult education, the Workers'
Educational Association, is an urban movement with comparatively
little influence in the villages; there is no corresponding movement for
advanced higher education in the countryside.

There are two obvious reasons for the less vigorous development
of education in the countryside – its inferior economic position, as
compared with the urban centres of industry, and the size and scattered
character of the villages which do not lend themselves to easy
organisation for the purposes of education and recreational life.

II Educationally the countryside is subordinate to the towns and its
schools are dominated by, and are subservient to, the urban system of
secondary and higher education. Owing to the operation of the
free-place scholarships system, the abler children are taken from the
country schools into the town secondary schools, where they receive
a predominantly literary and academic education under urban conditions divorced from the life and habits of the countryside. Either they
are lost to the villages and become town workers, or return to their
homes unfitted and untrained for life as countrymen and countrywomen. If, as seems possible, the number of urban secondary schools

is increased, and the proportion of free places is universally raised from 25 to 40 per cent, the plight of the countryside will be intensified. Already many education authorities, confronted with the demand for increased secondary education, are considering schemes for additional secondary and central schools in the towns to which country children are to be conveyed on a large scale by train and fleets of motor omnibuses.

With the realisation that the welfare of the countryside depends on 'better farming, better business, and better living', much is now being done by the state and by voluntary effort. But adult agricultural education, whether itinerant or centralised in residential colleges and farm institutes, the Women's Institute movement, rural libraries, village halls, rural community councils, admirable as they are, are not radical and comprehensive enough to bring about the reconstruction of the countryside.

III The need of the countryside will not be met until, by a recasting of the rural elementary school system, the villages are provided with an education, primary and secondary, which will fit boys and girls for life (in its widest sense) as countrymen and countrywomen;[1] until the countryside is provided with an institution in which the wide provisions of the great consolidated Education Act of 1921, especially in regard to higher and technical education, can be applied to and expressed in terms of rural life and industry; until the population of the countryside has guaranteed to it a social and recreational life based on stable foundations. This view is confirmed by that taken in the recently published *Final Report of the Agricultural Tribunal of Investigation*. In his review of the Report in the *Economic Journal* (September, 1924), Mr J. A. Venn, the Gilbey Lecturer in the History and Economics of Agriculture in the University of Cambridge, says:

The importance they (Sir William Ashley and Professor W. G. S. Adams) attach to education, using the word in its widest sense, will be seen when it is stated that, out of the forty-four recommendations contained in this part of the Report, no less than twenty-five are concerned with the means of organising the farmer and of improving his knowledge, not only of the industry itself, but also of its surroundings.

---

1 Such an education will not unfit them for life in any sphere, whether in the country or the town; or prevent those who are fitted from entering upon any form of higher education of an academic type; nor need the training given commit the error of being 'prematurely vocational'.

But if we wish to build up a rural civilisation that will have chronic vigour the first essential is that the countryside should have a localised and indigenous system of education in its own right beginning with the child in the primary school. Itinerant adult agricultural education, rural libraries and village halls will always be fighting a battle already half lost, if leaving the village system of elementary education as it is, we forget the children and the older boys and girls, and allow the ablest of them to be stolen by the secondary schools of the towns.

The problem of the village school

IV The first step towards providing the countryside with a more efficient education will lie in the reorganisation of the village schools into a system of senior or central schools in the larger villages, supported by tributary junior schools for children under the age of 11 in the smaller surrounding villages. The reasons in favour of such a policy are well known and need only be briefly recapitulated.

In Cambridgeshire for example there are 33 schools with an average attendance below 30, 14 schools with an average attendance between 30 and 40, 14 schools with an average attendance between 40 and 50, 12 schools with an average attendance between 50 and 60, and 41 schools with an average attendance between 60 and 100. Only 21 schools have an average attendance of between 100 and 250.

In these small schools all the children from 3 to 14 years of age are either housed in a single room or, if there is a separate classroom for the infants, all the children above standard 1 occupy the main room. The main room is sometimes divided by a curtain, less often by a screen. Children of varying ages and varying standards of attainment are necessarily grouped in a single class.

The older children perhaps suffer most – they mark time after the age of 11 or 12; the staff is not large enough to meet their special needs and, if it were, the equipment and accommodation for more advanced instruction is lacking.

In brief, the village school with an average attendance of 100 and under is not susceptible of organisation on any sound principle and the small numbers do not allow of the provision of the staff, accommodation and equipment, which make a wider curriculum possible. The small school is both inadequate and expensive.

V An illustration of what happens when the schools of an area are grouped in accordance with a plan is afforded in the Burwell area of

Cambridgeshire. In Burwell there were four schools, three voluntary schools and one council school, each working as a separate entity. One old church school was closed: the two other church schools were organised as junior schools for the children under 10 and the council school as a senior school for those over 10 years. The senior school was enlarged by the addition of a room for handicrafts and domestic subjects and land for a school garden was hired. Later, the older children from the neighbouring villages of Reach and Swaffham Prior were transferred to the Burwell Senior School.

At Burwell Senior School there are 150 children of 10–15 years of age. They are graded in classes according to age and attainment, each under the charge of a qualified teacher. Handicrafts, domestic subjects and gardening form an integral part of the training. Great importance is attached to the teaching of English (the school produces a play once a year), to local history and to physical training. There is a strong corporate life and there are thriving athletic and hobby clubs. The school has its colours, with a school cap for the boys, and a smock and cap for the girls. The children travelling from a distance take their midday meal together under the charge of a teacher.

VI The ultimate aim of the Cambridgeshire scheme is to establish some 30–40 senior or central schools under the charge of graduates or specially qualified head teachers. It is hoped then to concentrate all the older children of the county in these centres, and to give them there advanced instruction with a strong rural bias in schools adequately equipped and staffed. Three important results will follow. The numbers of older children in attendance at the senior schools will make possible the organisation of a class system in each school that will have regard to age and attainments. It will be possible to concentrate the facilities for handicrafts, domestic subjects, general elementary science, and gardening in a limited number of centres. At the same time the staffs at the tributary schools, relieved of the responsibility of the older children, will be able to devote themselves effectively to the needs of the infant and junior children.

The Cambridgeshire grouping scheme has had two interesting results:

(a) The senior schools have made it possible to attract a new type of teacher to the countryside. Apart from specially qualified teachers, there are now ten head and assistant teachers in Cambridgeshire who are graduates of Oxford, Cambridge, London, Glasgow, Wales and Birmingham.

(b) Owing to the difficulties inherent in the dual system of voluntary and council schools, the Education Committee set up an advisory committee representative of all denominations and of the teaching profession and presided over by the then Vice-Chancellor of the University (Dr E. C. Pearce, Master of Corpus Christi College) with the object of arriving at an agreed syllabus of religious teaching. The work of the committee was successful and resulted in what is known as the 'Cambridgeshire Concordat,' which includes the *Cambridgeshire Syllabus of Religious Teaching for Schools*[1]. Two Bibles based on the syllabus ('*The Little Children's Bible*' and '*The Children's Bible*'), edited by Professor Alexander Nairne, Sir Arthur Quiller-Couch, and Dr T. R. Glover have been published by the Cambridge University Press and are in use in Cambridgeshire schools. (The sales of the children's Bibles in Great Britain have reached 60,000 and an American edition has been published by Messrs Macmillan.)

VII The grouping of the schools of the countryside on the lines just described will have consequences of profound importance in rural England. In course of time the vast congeries of rural schools will be formed into an ordered system of two types of school, for those under eleven years or thereabouts and those over that age. With the assignment of a defined and comprehensible function to all the schools, there will accrue immense gains in organisation, in the economical provision of buildings and equipment, in the development and enrichment of the curriculum, and in the training of the teachers. Money will be saved and better spent. The system will be such as to allow, as and when circumstances demand, of the easy and natural development of centrally-situated rural secondary schools. There will at last be possible all over the English countryside a rural education of a secondary type for the training of boys and girls for life as countrymen and countrywomen.

The village college

VIII But if rural England is to have the education it needs and the social and recreational life it deserves, more is required than the reorganisation of the elementary school system; and that which is required is possible.

There must be a grouping and co-ordination of all the educational and social agencies, whether statutory or voluntary, which now exist

---

1 Published by Cambridge University Press.

in isolation in the countryside; an amalgamation which, while pre-serving the individuality and function of each, will assemble them into a whole and make possible their expression for the first time in a new institution, single but many-sided, for the countryside.

IX What this means may be shown in detail.

The county council is the statutory authority for:

(i) Education:
   Elementary
   Higher
   (a) Secondary education and day continuation schools
   (b) Further education
   (c) Agricultural education
   Social and physical training for children, young persons, and adults
(ii) The Public Libraries Act, 1919
(iii) Juvenile Employment and Unemployment Insurance
(iv) Public Health
(v) Agriculture (including the lesser rural industries).

The county council is therefore the statutory authority for the whole of the legislation which provides for the social and economic welfare of the countryside by means of educational, recreational and community facilities[1], except that in regard to the two latter, its powers are shared by the rural district and parish councils. But the functions of the major statutory authority are carried out in separation in the village, and there is no co-ordination of county council services with those of the minor local authority. The main reason for this is that the village elementary school is not adequate to the wide conception of education as covering all ages and activities and including social and physical training as it is expressed in the consolidated Education Act of 1921. In most, if not all, villages there will be found, side by side with a piece of elementary education, a group of evening classes held in the elementary school if no other building is available. There may be a Women's Institute class and a British Legion class; a choral class in a private house; and one or two agricultural education classes held either in the school, or in the parish hall, or in a barn or other farm building. The branch of the

1 By community facilities are meant parochial buildings for non-ecclesiastical purposes, recreation grounds, etc., and not services provided, e.g. by the Rural District Council as the 'sanitary authority'.

2 An almost universal need is felt in the villages for a worthy home for the library, with room for reading during the long winter evenings when the small cottage is filled by the family and the light is none too good for reading.

county library has no appropriate home – it is housed in a corner of the school or hall or in a private residence[2]. The recreation ground belonging to the Parish Council is stationed in an outlying corner of the village. If there is an infant welfare centre, that is housed in another corner.

The existing activities are not only carried on in isolation from one another, but the greater number are not suitably accommodated. Again, the existing elementary school building does not allow of the development of fuller educational facilities for young people and adults. Finally, if there is no suitable village hall, the voluntary associations of the countryside have no place in which to meet except the children's school; there a large number of social gatherings must be held; and there even accommodation for the work of village local government must by law be found rent free.

X All the activities and facilities that already exist in the countryside and all those which by statute could be provided, should be brought together in and around one institution. In Cambridgeshire the aim would be to establish in about ten carefully selected centres where senior schools are already organised, a system of village colleges which would provide for the co-ordination and development of all forms of education – primary, secondary, further and adult education, including agricultural education – together with social and recreational facilities, and at the same time furnish a community centre in the fullest sense of the neighbourhood.

In these centres the isolated elementary school as such, with all the narrower conceptions associated with it, would be abolished; it would be absorbed into a larger institution.

Let us, for sake of illustration, visualise the village college as consisting of two wings or three-sided courts, one containing the school portion, the other accommodation specially set apart for adult activities, and with the village hall between, thus:

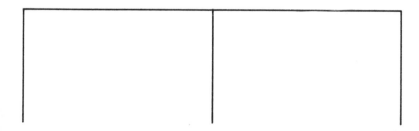

The village college would provide for the following:

(1) A nursery schoolroom which would also serve for use as an infant welfare centre.

(2) A primary school for the children of 5–10 years of age of the central village only.

(3) A school providing a rural education of a secondary type for children from 10–15 or 16 years in the central village and the tributary villages of the chosen area. Such tributary villages would be within reasonable walking or cycling or train or motor-omnibus distance (on the average 2–3½ miles in Cambridgeshire); and the tributary villages would retain a junior school for infants and juniors up to the age of 10 years. The school thus forming part of the village college would in addition to classrooms contain a workshop for handicrafts, a room for domestic science (cookery, laundry, housewifery, etc.) and a room for general elementary science. These three rooms would also be used for evening adult education in crafts, domestic subjects and agricultural science.

(4) A staff room for teachers, a room for the work of the school medical service, and the usual offices for teachers and children.

(5) The village hall, which would serve for use

(a) in the day, as a school assembly hall, for the midday meal, school functions, physical training and school plays and concerts;

(b) in the evenings, for broadcast programmes at stated hours, concerts, performances by the village dramatic and musical societies, exhibitions by the travelling cinema of the Cambridgeshire Rural Community Council, lectures, dances, whist drives and public meetings.

(6) A room divided into two parts – a library section containing a permanent nucleus of books and the monthly supply of books from the Cambridgeshire County Library, where villagers could read and study in peace and reasonable comfort; and a reading-room section containing newspapers and periodicals.

The library would thus be intimately associated with every stage and type of educational work carried on in the college, and would be used by every student from the youngest to the oldest. A new conception, the public library, as that department which provides the educational tool known as 'books', would be realised. Schoolboys and girls, their older sisters and brothers, and their parents would freely pass to and fro between classroom or lecture-room or the demonstration plot and the library.

(7) A room definitely set apart for agricultural education, containing

maps, charts and specimens, to be used jointly with the science laboratory (Paragraph (3)).

Such a room with the laboratory would provide for the theoretical portion of that type of agricultural education – local courses and local instruction – which in accordance with the scheme of the Ministry of Agriculture does not come within the scope of the Farm Institute. The village college would also be the natural centre near which instruction in manual processes such as thatching, hedging and ditching and the use of agricultural machinery, would take place, and demonstrations given in veterinary science and farriery; and where technical instruction and advice on rural industries would be available.

The demonstrations of crops would be organised at farms near the village college. In Cambridgeshire all demonstrations carried out by the agricultural education sub-committee of the education committee would thus be concentrated in village college centres, and could be co-ordinated with the work of the school and also with the adult agricultural courses given in the college. The village college would then form a centre for agricultural and horticultural education.

(8) Two or more rooms;

(a) primarily to provide appropriate accommodation for adult education, particularly in humane subjects, and for the more informal adult educational activities such as study circles, debating societies, dramatic and musical societies;

(b) accommodation for village meetings connected with the Women's Institutes, the British Legion, Boy Scouts and Girl Guides, and committee meetings connected with village activities such as the Horticultural and Flower Show, the Summer Festival and Athletic Sports, the Village Football, Cricket and Tennis Clubs, and

(c) for such activities of rural local government as must by law be accommodated in a public elementary school if no other public building is available, e.g. parish council meetings, local government inquiries, meetings under the Allotment Acts; candidature for persons for either district or parish councils, any parish or local government committees appointed to administer public funds and endowments within the parish (Local Government Act 1894, Sect. 4).

(9) Simple shower baths and a dressing room (both in a basement) for the use of the school children, and of the athletic clubs of the village. (Village athletes hardly ever enjoy the luxury of a hot bath and rub-down after the game!)

(10) The village recreation ground provided by the parish council

alongside. This would provide additional playing-field accommodation without extra cost for all the children at the school, and would take the place of the old asphalt or concrete schoolyard.

(11) A plot of ground to serve for a school garden, and for the smaller demonstrations in horticulture.

(12) A centre for carrying out the education authority's work connected with choice of employment and juvenile unemployment insurance.

(13) A centre for lectures, evening classes, and education in all matters affecting public health.

(14) The warden's house

(15) Accommodation for indoor recreations. There is nothing to prevent the local education authority renting the rooms of a county council building for recreational purposes, such as clubs and games. And it should not be forgotten that the local education authority have powers under Section 86 of the Education Act, 1921, to provide facilities for social and physical training for children, young persons, and adults. But a centre such as that in which the village college is situated might reasonably and naturally require accommodation explicitly set apart for indoor games, especially billiards, and controlled by village trustees.

It is important and essential that the accommodation for such indoor recreations should not be disassociated from the village college, if that institution is to realise its functions as a community centre for the area – educational and social.

The following is put forward as a perfectly satisfactory solution of this problem:

(a) As in the case of many central and secondary schools the school buildings or other part of the village college could be utilised in the evenings for boys' and girls' clubs, the Debating Society, the Chess Club, and Dramatic Club, the Natural History Club, the Photography Club, and indoor games.

(b) The block containing a billiard room and one or more small rooms for the various indoor games could be built adjacent to the college. The two buildings need only be separated by a few yards; they would be actively associated in use in daily life and habit, though administratively they would be separate entities.

Such recreation rooms would be provided out of voluntary funds; or if thus associated with a village college they might be made eligible for a grant from any funds set aside for the purpose by the Development Commissioners and the Ministry of Agriculture. They would be under proper control, i.e. of trustees consisting of the village social council.

(c) On the other hand, there is nothing to prevent the recreation rooms expressly forming a part of the village college; and it would be interesting if the Development Commissioners and the Ministry of Agriculture, co-operating with the Board of Education and the local education authority (regard being had to the latter's powers under Section 86 of the Education Act, 1921) followed out this plan for experimental purposes if a village college is established in Cambridgeshire.

It should be noted that a building serving all the needs enumerated in Paragraphs (1)–(15) can be provided and maintained by the Statutory Authority.

All that part concerning elementary and higher education (including school garden and playground) would rank for grant from the Board of Education. All the services of elementary and higher education carried on within its walls would be statutory service provided and maintained by the local authority and aided by the Board of Education.

The services of agricultural education would be eligible for the $66\frac{2}{3}$ per cent maintenance grants of the Ministry of Agriculture who also have power to contribute a grant of 75 per cent towards the capital cost of any part of the building not eligible for grant from the Board of Education and used primarily for agricultural education for persons over the age of 16 years.

The capital cost and the maintenance of the library and reading-room section of the building would be a rate aided service only, except in so far as it might be possible for the Board of Education and the Ministry of Agriculture to contribute to the capital cost and maintenance on account of work done in connection with elementary and higher and agricultural education. (See Paragraph (6) above.)

The hall portion would be eligible for the grant of the Board of Education as it would be an integral part of the school and would be available for social and physical training under Section 86 of the Education Act of 1921.

In this connection the assistance of the Ministry of Agriculture and the Development Commissioners who are considering the question of grants to village halls might be enlisted.

It may be noted that in all villages the premises of council schools which are the property of the local authority are rented for general purposes when not required for educational purposes; and this would apply to village colleges.

The recreation ground is a service provided by the parish council; associated with it might be any land provided by the education authority as a playing-field under Section 86 of the Education Act of 1921.

XI Government The control of the village college would be vested in a body of governors responsible to the local authority, consisting of:

(a) The managers of the school. As the school would serve more than one village, such a body would by statute be a composite body consisting of managers appointed by the county council, and managers appointed by the minor local authorities of the area served.

(b) Members appointed by the county council as representing local interests, including the voluntary associations concerned with educational and social activities, to supervise higher, including agricultural, education. The parish councils (or parish meetings) as statutory minor local authorities for elementary education might appropriately be associated with the supervision of higher education.

(c) A representative appointed by the Senate of the University of Cambridge.

(d) Representatives of other interests, e.g. the parish council as owners of the recreation ground.

The body of governors would be appointed under an approved scheme providing for the proper discharge of statutory functions. The body of governors when acting as a whole would act in an advisory and consultative capacity only except when they might as a whole properly act executively as, for example, in regard to all forms of higher education. Executive acts in regard to certain other services would devolve on the constituent section statutorily responsible as, for example, in the case of the elementary school on the managers. The governing body in so far as it carried out services for which the county council is the local authority would be responsible to the county council.

XII Head of the village college. The head of the village college following on the co-ordination of educational services would combine several functions. A new type of leader and teacher with a higher status and of superior calibre would at last be possible in the English countryside. An appropriate title expressing this new status and wider scope is therefore required. He might be styled the Warden – we should read then of the Warden of Sawston; the Warden of Bourn; and why not Provost, or Master, or Principal in some cases.

He would have to be a man country-bred and trained at a University; a Science Degree would be an additional qualification;

above all he would have to be a man with a love of and understanding of rural life, with powers of leadership.

As Headmaster of the school he would be entitled to the appropriate salary under the allocated standard scale; in addition he would be paid sums for duties supervisory and otherwise in connection with higher education.

The scope of the warden's duties, the amount of his remuneration and the allocation of proportions of it, e.g. to elementary education (or to secondary education if the school within the college is designed to comply with the regulations for secondary schools), further education (and perhaps agricultural education), are questions that require more detailed treatment than is possible in this brief memorandum. The problem is one that would best be stated not in the abstract, but when specific proposals for a village college are formulated to the Board of Education (and the Ministry of Agriculture).

XIII Relation to voluntary associations

Important considerations arise in connection with the relation of the village college to the voluntary associations of the countryside. The whole welfare of communities, and the vigour and prosperity of their social life in particular, depend on the extent to which centres of unfettered initiative can be developed within them – that is, on freedom. The object of the village college, therefore, will be to enhance, and not to diminish, the freedom and initiative of the voluntary associations of the countryside; and there need be no kind of principle involved in its organisation and scope that will conflict with this side of its function.

There are three main aspects under which the relation of the village college to voluntary associations requires to be considered:

(a) *Government* The voluntary associations whose scope includes educational and social welfare will have direct representation on the governing body of the village college (Paragraph XI on Government, Section (b)).

(b) *The head of the village college* The executive functions of the head of the village college (exercised under the supervision of the governing body) will be confined to educational services for which the statutory authority is responsible. But he would, of course, take an important part in the larger life of the community, in the spirit of the words 'I stand amongst you as he that serveth.'

(c) *Assistance to voluntary associations* There will be two chief ways in which the village college will be called upon to assist voluntary associations.

First, when the voluntary association desires educational facilities that can be provided by the statutory authority. Certain administrative conditions concerned mainly with the standard of instruction and the number and attendance of pupils being complied with, such educational facilities will be provided without any interference with the independence of the voluntary association. The situation in this case will be, not that the members of a voluntary organisation are attending a class organised by the statutory authority, but that all the facilities that the statutory authority can offer are being used in connection with a class initiated by a voluntary association, attended mainly by members of the voluntary association, and supervised by them.

Secondly, when the voluntary association desires accommodation or other facilities at the village college.

In both these cases the voluntary associations will lay their requests before the governing body, on which the voluntary associations will be directly represented; such educational facilities as are available will be granted; and an allocation will be made of the accommodation either for longer or shorter periods, or in respect of particular evenings. The authority's regulations for the letting of their premises, in which a differentiation is made between the type of meeting for which no rent is charged and that for which a rent is charged, will apply.

The village college will thus associate the voluntary associations of the countryside with the administration of statutory services, so that these benefits may be fully appropriated by the community, and supply more effectively adjusted to demand. Where there is no public vision, the statutory authority perisheth; and this contact between the statutory authority with its many powers, and the impulse and enthusiasm of voluntary associations will have many beneficent results.

More important still, the village college will provide a theatre for the free and unfettered activities of the voluntary associations. The village college will be the surest guarantee of their welfare and vigour. At the same time, without doing violence to freedom, some unity in the life of the rural community will be attained.

XIV Architecture The possibility of bringing together all the various educational and social services that would find a habitation within the village college, and of achieving this remarkable synthesis depends in the first place on the provision of an appropriate building.

The building that will form the village college will be so new in English Architecture, and its significance so great, that the design and construction of the first village colleges should be very carefully provided for. For we are in measurable sight, if we use imagination and have administrative courage, of giving to the English countryside a number of fine and worthy public buildings. The schools of rural England are nearly always bad and seldom beautiful – never a form of art, as they might and ought to be. The greater portion of them were designed to serve the joint purpose of a school and parish hall, and at a time when the standard of staffing and accommodation, the quality of the curriculum and the conception of teaching were vastly inferior to those of our own day. As the Education Act of 1921 is progressively put into operation, the buildings are bound to be replaced; large numbers of new educational buildings costing large sums of money will spring up in England and Wales, and the process will be accelerated if, as seems possible, the system of 'dual control' of voluntary and council schools is abolished within the lifetime of the present government. There is no reason why the erection of these new buildings should not be made the opportunity of adding to the public architecture of the countryside; and there is additional reason that the opportunity should not be missed because there is not likely ever to be any other constructive movement so national and widespread, so completely affecting the lives of the whole community, as that of public education. The provision of buildings for the system of public education will in the present century be one of the chiefest ways in which the art of architecture can influence the body politic. If the opportunity is not taken it will only be through dullness and lack of courage.

The difference between good and bad architecture is more often the difference between a good design and a bad design, than the difference between cheap and costly material. Assuming that good material will be available for a village college, the important thing is to see that it has a significant design. Such a design must be simple, but it could be beautiful. Using our imagination, let us say to the architect: 'Education is one of our greatest public services and one of the most widely diffused. Every year we spend on it some 80 millions. Every town and every village must have its educational buildings. Education touches every citizen. We have a conception of a new institution for the countryside, an institution that will touch every side of the life of the inhabitants of the district in which it is placed. Will you think out a design for such a building, a village college? A building that will express the spirit of the English countryside which it is intended to grace, something of its humaneness and modesty, something of the age-long and permanent dignity of husbandry; a building that will give the countryside a centre of reference arousing the affection and loyalty of the country child and country people, and conferring significance on their way of life? If this can be done simply and effectually, and the varying needs which the village college will serve realised as an entity and epitomised in a building, a standard may be set and a great tradition may be begun; in such a synthesis architecture will find a fresh and widespread means of expression. If the village college is a true and workable conception, the institution will, with various modifications, speed over rural England; and in course of time a new series of worthy public buildings will stand side by side with the parish churches of the countryside.'

XV The village college as thus outlined would not create something superfluous; it would not be a spectacular experiment and a costly luxury. It would take all the various vital but isolated activities in village life – the school, the village hall and reading room, the evening classes, the agricultural education courses, the Women's Institute, the British Legion, Boy Scouts and Girl Guides, the recreation ground, the branch of the county rural library, the athletic and recreation clubs, the work of village local government – and, bringing them together into relation, create a new institution for the English countryside. It would create out of discrete elements an organic whole; the vitality and freedom of the constituent elements would be preserved, and not destroyed, but the unity they would form would be a new thing. For, as in the case of all organic unities, the whole is greater than the mere sum of the parts. It would be a true social synthesis – it would take existing and live elements and bring them into a new and unique relationship.

§ The village college would change the whole face of the problem of rural education. The isolated and insulated school, which has now no organic connection with higher education, would form part of an institution in which the ultimate goal of education would be realised. As the community centre of the neighbourhood the village college would provide for the whole man, and abolish the duality of education and ordinary life. It would not only be the training ground for the art of living, but the place in which life is lived, the environment of a genuine corporate life. The dismal dispute of vocational and non-vocational education would not arise in it, because education and living would be equated. It would be a visible demonstration in stone of the continuity and never ceasingness of education. There would be no 'leaving school'! – the child would enter at three and leave the college only in extreme old age[1]. It would have the great virtue of being local so that it would enhance the quality of actual life as it is lived from day to day – the supreme object of education. Unlike non-local residential institutions (the public schools, the universities, the few residential workingmen's colleges, and, to take a continental example, the Danish High Schools) it would not be divorced from the normal environment of those who would frequent it from day to day, or from that greater educational institution, the family. Has there ever been an educational institution that at one and the same time provided for the needs of the whole family and consolidated its life – its social physical, intellectual and economic life? Our modern educational institutions provide only for units of the family, or separate the individual from the family by time and space so that they may educate it apart and under less natural conditions. The village college would lie athwart the daily lives of the community it served; and in it the conditions would be realised under which education would be not an escape from reality, but an enrichment and transformation of it. For education is committed to the view that the ideal order and the actual order can ultimately be made one.

§ We are witnessing in this country through the extension of the principle of ownership the partial disappearance of the old landowners[2]. There are social, as well as economic problems, arising out of this change. The responsibilities of leadership and the maintenance of liberal and humane traditions in our squireless villages (which are the rule not the exception in Cambridgeshire) will fall on a larger number of shoulders – they will fall on the whole community. The village college will be the seat and guardian of humane public traditions in the countryside, the training ground of a rural democracy realising its social and political duties. Without some such institution as the village college a rural community consisting largely of agricultural workers, small proprietors and small farmers will not be equal to the task of maintaining a worthy rural civilisation. The alternative would be a countryside like that in some continental countries, prosperous perhaps, but narrow and materialistic, without native distinction and charm, and with no instinct for even the popular arts.

§ The village college, by linking up the local representatives of the county authority with the minor local authorities and uniting them in the concrete task of administering a many-sided local institution and

1 In all seriousness it might be said that the 'school leaving age' would be lifted to 90.
2 See a speech on this subject by the Minister for Agriculture (Mr. Edward Wood), *The Times* 10 December 1924.

powers visibly affecting the life around them from day to day, would revitalise rural local government. The parish council, still exercising its own powers, but concerned in the exercise of larger ones, would be endowed with new life. Good government and self government might at last be combined in the countryside. Rural local government languishes because there is no institution that provides a centre of reference and a means of expression. The village college would meet that need.

§ The village college would provide the chance for creating for the countryside a new type of village leader and teacher with a new status and a wide function embracing human welfare in its biggest sense – spiritual, physical, social and economic.

§ The village college would provide an opportunity for creative architecture. Our state system of education has not yet produced noble architecture on the same scale as that of all the other great movements of the national spirit. And there has been no public architecture in the English countryside since the parish churches were built – that is, since the Middle Ages. Apart from these inheritances from a past age, the biggest and most impressive public buildings in the countryside are the asylums and the workhouses; big asylums and poor schools – a sight to put all heaven in a rage.

§ The village college would have in it all the conditions of permanence. It will be formed by welding together existing institutions already planted deep in the habits and affections of the people. Its activities will have statutory authority, and statutory financial support, and its financial stability is therefore guaranteed.

§ Finally, the village college would not outlive its function, for the main reason that it would not be committed irrevocably to any intellectual or social dogma or to any sectional point of view. Intellectually it might be one of the freest of our English institutions.

The suggested plan for Cambridgeshire

XVI The County of Cambridge has already been mapped out in a series of about 30–40 areas which should be served by senior schools; and on an examination of the areas it appears that there are ten centres at which village colleges could be effectively organised. These centres are:

Sawston	Burwell
Bourn	Cottenham
Harston	Waterbeach
Linton	Weston Colville
Melbourn	Steeple Morden

These centres have been provisionally chosen because they dominate a suitably large and homogeneous area.

An immediate opportunity of establishing two village colleges on an experimental basis has now arisen at Sawston and Bourn. Each of the areas surrounding these two villages presents different features, and would require secondary modifications of the general plan of the village college to fit in with local conditions.

SAWSTON. The population of Sawston is 1,530. In addition to agriculture there is an important rural industry – the heating of pelts, which are converted into chamois leather for domestic use and for gloves. There is also a paper mill belonging to Spicers Ltd., and employing upwards of 300, where machine-papers of all the better grades are produced, and where the highest quality of currency and stamp paper is made. Considerable development of these works is in progress. The neighbouring villages are Whittlesford (population 980), Babraham (population 238), Pampisford (population 255) and Duxford (population 734). These villages are predominantly agricultural, except Whittlesford, which contributes workers to a paper mill and to a works for making agricultural implements.

The school at Sawston is a council school with an average attendance of 227 and already serves the purpose of a senior school for a portion of the district.

It occupies a commodius site which could, if necessary, be sold and the proceeds devoted to the purchase of a large site abutting on the recreation ground. The village has no hall at present, though some funds have been collected. A village college at Sawston would be able to provide effectively for the needs of the rural community of an area of five square miles and including typically agricultural villages such as Babraham, Pampisford and Duxford. Such an institution would provide for:

(a) A nursery, infants', and junior school for Sawston only.
(b) A rural school for the children of 10 years to 15 years of Sawston, Whittlesford, Babraham, Pampisford and Duxford.
(c) A community centre for Sawston.
(d) A centre of further adult and agricultural education for the area of Sawston, Whittlesford, Babraham, Pampisford and Duxford.

BOURN. Bourn (population 623) lies at the centre of a tract of purely agricultural country containing the villages of Caxton (population 398), Longstowe (population 249), Kingston (population 173), Caldecote (population 161) and Toft (population 205).

A village college at Bourn would follow the general lines of the college at Sawston. The area is very poorly served both with educational and social facilities, and there would be an opportunity of showing the maximum effect that a composite institution like the village college would have on the educational, social, and economic life of a population wholly engaged in agricultural pursuits. At Bourn it would be possible to make the village college the centre of agricultural education and demonstration for young men and women and adults in the surrounding area.

Conclusion: Cambridgeshire as a demonstration area for rural reconstruction

XVII The steps by which two experimental examples of a village college could be established in Sawston and Bourn have now been described. But the compact rural County of Cambridgeshire affords a tract of England in which a system of village colleges might be established. Here is Cambridgeshire wholly agricultural with its representative agricultural community; the university in the middle with the great department of agricultural and horticultural research, and the National Institute of Agricultural Botany; its scheme for grouping rural schools and fashioning an efficient system of rural education; a county system of agricultural and horticultural education; a scheme of rural adult education in working order; a progressive policy of public health; its county rural library with a branch in every village; its rural community council working with the assistance of the experts of various departments of the university; its council of musical education and musical festival.

Picture it with its educational, economic and social life reborn by a system of village colleges, starting with Sawston and Bourn, and gradually increased to about ten. If the Carnegie Trustees and the Development Commissioners could father such a scheme, they might perform a work of reconstruction of first-rate national importance. The possibilities are so great that they do not require stressing. The Trustees might initiate an educational advance which would be one of the greatest in the history of state education. They might make possible at last after a generation of discussion a really massive contribution to the rural problem which it could be said without exaggeration would surpass anything that has been done in any country, more comprehensive for instance than the Consolidated Rural Schools of the United States, or the Rural High Schools of Denmark.

One swallow does not make a summer; and a single college at Sawston or at Bourn, though it might mark a turning point, would not afford the palpable and concrete demonstration of rural reconstruction as would a tract of rural England like Cambridgeshire its whole life re-orientated by a system of village colleges.

The time is ripe for a great constructive step forward in the rural problem. The work of re-establishing the life and welfare of the countryside is admitted to be really urgent; it is required in the interests of our national life and health. And as we may not always remain predominantly an industrial country, it is necessary that the problem of the reconstruction of the village should be dealt with in good time. There are certain economic aspects of rural welfare that can only be dealt with by governments; but all the other aspects of the rural welfare are such as can be dealt with by education in its widest sense and by the rebuilding of the social life of the countryside.

And if this great work cannot be carried out in accordance with some such plan as has been briefly described, in what way is it possible to conceive its ever being done?

2

Institutionalism and Freedom in Education

Introduction

It must have seemed strange for a chief education officer of a strongly conservative local authority to be writing for a journal which was a supporter of 'progressive schools' and known for its radical ideas. It is however an indication of Morris's own radical ideas that he agreed to write for the *New Ideals Quarterly*. The resulting article contains some of his most profound thoughts about the future of education, while at the same time readers may no doubt notice some questionable assertions. Also it may be felt that the article deals less satisfactorily with the subject indicated by its title than with the new ideals in education which he was keen to expound.

Again it may have surprised regular readers of the journal at the time to be told that education is undetachable from religion, that it is, or should be, 'an induction into a way of life', and to have it pointed out that the Roman Catholic Church was once the most potent educational force in the Western world, when it was able to 'assemble and marshall the temporal order of society under the sanctions of eternity, thus redeeming the episode of life on one of the humblest of the planets from triviality, ruin and despair.' He goes on to compare the great achievement of the Church with the 'spiritual futility' of our state system of education, and at the same time deplores the lapse into individualism which has accompanied the 'secularisation of life', and the disappearance of the 'great positive political conception of the community'.

He recognises and states most clearly that it is not possible to put back the clock and resurrect the religion of the past; he then proceeds to map out his own answer to our deplorable condition by giving a new role and a new meaning to education. In doing so he condemns the existing system which 'does not concern itself actively with the adult life of man, with his political and social welfare and his ultimate desires and hopes, his destiny and significance'.

Turning the coin he adds a paragraph where, with almost lyrical disapproval, he castigates the concentration of schooling on the young and, with it, teacher training, professors of education, higher education and the Board of Education. His own recipe is manifold. Education should be 'conterminous with life'. – 'We must do away with the insulated school', our places of education should be 'centres of corporate life and not congeries of classrooms for discourse and instruction'. The main concern of education should be 'the life that the adult will lead, the working philosophy by which he will live, the politics of the community which he will serve in his maturity'.

In the final pages of the article he turns to the subject indicated by the title.

Here he defends himself against the suggestion that a government, through legislation or through its agents, the teachers, might become dominant and dominating; a threat to democracy. He sees the solution in the limiting of government power mostly to the provision of *facilities* for education and recreation, these latter being provided by 'autonomous societies' (for example the W.E.A. or the universities). If his argument here seems weak today, his determination to ward off dictatorship of any kind is strongly expressed, as when he writes: 'The whole welfare of communities and the vigour and prosperity of their intellectual and social life depends on the extent to which centres of unfettered initiative can be developed within them.' As for the threat from teachers, he maintains that by releasing them from the prison house of the school, they will become much less narrowly professional, indeed, much better educated. 'It is only in a world where education is confined to infants and adolescents...that the teacher is liable to become a pundit or a tyrant.'

Institutionalism and Freedom in Education

Article in 'New Ideals Quarterly' issued by the Committee of New Ideals in Education, Vol. Two, No. One, March 1926

During the past two years there has been a revival of the discussions with regard to religious education, because it has become clear that there can be no great constructive advance in the organization of educational facilities until the administrative problem of dual control is settled. I do not wish, even for a moment, to enter into any of the phases of that vexed question except to observe that there has arisen a definite realization on all sides that there is a communal side to education; that education is not only the dissemination of knowledge, but an induction into a way of life; that discursive reason operating in separation from will and the emotions is common to the evil man and the good man, and is too often a disruptive and disintegrating force; that it is as members of a community that the life of action and conduct is best realized and our souls saved; and that the state system of education functioning in an atmosphere of neutrality may become the expression of the lowest common denominator of life, a mere ante-chamber of the human spirit, incapable of communicating a sense of the significance of life, of creating traditions, and stimulating loyalties, destitute of beauty and architecture.

And the fears are all the more justified because the development of the state system of education in England as well as of representative government during the nineteenth and the present centuries has taken place side by side with a shrinkage in the authority and influence of the great religious and social institutions which sometimes guided life and governed conduct. This latter process had indeed been going on in our country since the breakdown of the Catholic system – the greatest synthesis, it has been said by a modern naturalist, of instinct, mind and conduct that has even been achieved in Europe.

Our state system of education, whatever else it may be, has not been the creation of a great religious organization with a philosophy comprehending life and death, and with sublime beliefs about man and his place in the universe. The Catholic system created and nourished a civilization – the National Society was founded to 'educate the children of the poor in the principles of the Established Church'; the juxtaposition of those two statements helps one to understand what a change in the conceptions of the relation of religion to education and of education to the community has taken place in this country since the sixteenth century. The effects of the disintegration and secularization of life are to be seen on every hand, especially in the profound spiritual futility of our state system of education.

Other effects are to be seen in the individualism of large numbers of educated people, and in those urban conglomerations produced by the industrial revolution, many of whose inhabitants seem only to be known to the rent collector and the undertaker.

The state system of education has, therefore, arisen in a period of intellectual and political confusion. It has been divorced and is increasingly divorced from a great imaginative conception of the significance and destiny of human life, and has not been nourished by a great positive political conception of the community. It has lacked religion and institutionalism and civic inspiration. It has been confined to a class and has not served the whole community; it has been effectively cut off from the universities, and its teachers recruited almost wholly from one class and educated in pedagogical seminaries, cut off from the main centres of higher education. Education has come to mean the education of the very young and has been confined to the school. As there has been no developed system of adult education, the education of the young and the training of the teachers has been carried on without any adequate realization of the ultimate goal of education.

For the greatest and most difficult task educators could have, and the primary task of education, is to construct the world of the youth and adult, and to give them faith to live in it and competence to cope with it.

I do not think we can look forward to the arising of another great all-embracing religious organization like the Catholic Church that will assemble and marshal the temporal order of society under the sanctions of eternity, thus redeeming the episode of life on one of the humblest of the planets from triviality, ruin and despair. Much less, the English temperament and mind being what it is, can we hope or wish that we should be saved by the device of the worship of the visible state, whether conceived in Germany or elsewhere.

And yet, we who are educationists, to use a convenient but unattractive word, cannot acquiesce in a secular education, meaning by that an education which is utilitarian, which is merely departmental, which concerns itself merely with efficiency, which does not concern itself with and shape and influence the activities, hopes, and fears of adult human life, which is not the movement that affects the whole human career, which is but one word for health, science, art, politics, morality, and religion.

It is the life that the adult will lead, the working philosophy by which he will live, the politics of the community which he will serve in his maturity, that should be the main concern of education. Unless education is concerned with these, frames the values, influences them and adumbrates them, then the education of the young will be in vain. For the training of the very young is largely preventive medicine; and its effectiveness almost wholly depends on the ultimate values and the conception of the goal of education which exists in the mind of the teacher, and into which the child will, in due course, be inducted.

When an educational system is divorced from philosophy, when it does not concern itself actively with the adult life of man, with his political and social welfare, and his ultimate desires and hopes, his destiny and significance, what do we get?

A system concerning itself almost wholly with the young, to whom the greater part of human experience and achievement is necessarily non-existent; teachers of the young habituated to a childish world from the subject-matter of which three-fourths of reality is quite inevitably abstracted; a disproportionate emphasis on methods of imparting information and the intensive analysis of the subject-matter of curricula; training colleges which are not primarily microcosms of life and places of liberal culture but institutions for the study of the formal apparatus of the teaching process; professors of education instead of men and women who are teachers and educators because they are first thinkers and prophets and artists; the school divorced from higher education, and higher education divorced on the whole from government, industry, from creation of all kinds, from play and love and tragedy, from religion and art and discourse. We are inundated with child psychology; the administrative system of our local authorities is refined to perfection, and the great central administration in London concerns itself with the quantitative side of education; we have conferences of directors of education which ought to be conferences of philosophers, meeting interminably to discuss the statutory rules and orders of the Board of Education and the anomalies of the grant system. And side by side with this we witness a signal failure in cities and the countryside to achieve the art of living, and a profound secularism exhibiting itself in the cynicism of the fortunate and the purposelessness of those whom society treats as means and not as ends. Walk through a city on a Saturday night, or through a country town or a village, and see for yourselves how little our state system of education is doing to help the multitudes to live a life worth living or even to enjoy their leisure. Think of the partial failure of representative government, of the fantastic orgy called a general election, and of the ignorance and consequent weakness of local government on which the effective working of all our social and remedial legislation depends.

I have said that I think there are no signs of a religious organization arising with a synthesis of instinct, life and conduct that would dominate education, which would itself be the great educator; or that the visible state with its objects, political and otherwise, will in England become the end of education, harnessing the educational system to itself. I do not wish to discuss whether these possibilities are desirable. I want to discuss what I think is actually happening, what in the nature of things must happen, the way in which we can construct an educational system in harmony both with circumstances, and, those circumstances being what they are, with what we should wish in our hearts education at the least to be.

The first need is that we should reconstruct our conception of education and the system by which it is to be realized so that it will be conterminous with life. Education should be the impulse and the method by which the community in all directions realizes the best life for itself. At the present moment our state system is concerned almost wholly with children and the teachers of children. We ought to see our way to the organic provision of education for the whole adult community. We must do away with the insulated school. We must so organize the educational buildings of the towns and countryside that the schools of the young are either organically related to or form part of institutions in which the ultimate goals of education are realized. This is as important for the teaching of the young as it is for the teachers themselves. Then we must associate with education all these activities which go to make a full life – art, literature, music, recreation, festivals, local government, politics. We must institutionalize our places of education so that they become centres of corporate life and not congeries of classrooms for discourse and instruction. We should picture a town or a village clustering round its educational buildings, with its hall, library, and recreation grounds, where young and old not only acquire knowledge but are inducted into a way of life. In such institutions touching every side of the lives of the inhabitants of the town or the village, some unity in the life of the community would be attained, and the duality of education and living abolished. The institution, and the activities within it, would become a microcosm of life, not merely a place in which instruction is imparted by a body of specialists, but a place in which the community endeavours to realize the highest sum of good life.

I trust that this does not sound like an aimless and impracticable dream. Remember that one or more of the tendencies, which I urge should be expressed as a whole in our state system, have been realized in separation in our varied educational institutions. What we require is the imagination and the will to achieve within the state system a synthesis of forces and tendencies that already exist.

No doubt the work will seem well nigh impossible in our large cities. In these cities some success has already been attained in securing some kind of unity in the educational institutions which they possess, though we must not be content with mere unity of administration or the semi–organic unity which comes by linking up the primary schools with the secondary schools, and the secondary schools with higher education, and the university of the area. In our new towns an attempt is being made successfully to associate the activities of adult life with the more strictly educational activities, to found institutions which will provide the means of a liberal life. In our own county of Cambridgeshire we hope soon to demonstrate how the whole educational, social and economic life of a community can be provided for in an institution which is to be called the Village College.

What I have been urging in this paper is that we should abolish the barriers which separate education from all those activities which make up adult living; that it should be the first duty of education to concern itself with the ultimate goals of education as they exist for the manhood and womanhood of the community; that the activity we call education should mean the attempt, critical and constructive, to increase the sum and enhance the quality of good life; that this activity should not only concern man as an economic and political animal, but should be the means whereby the life of the community is conserved and consecrated, and the individual's sense of the significance and destiny of human life kept alive and intact. Man's life as an economic, social, and religious animal – that is the subject-matter of education, and education the means whereby he achieves the best in all these respects.

If education were conceived of as such, and actively realized and organized as such in the life of any community, the teachers would become our leaders, the makers or breakers of a nation. It might be objected that a power greater than that ever dreamed of by any church would be placed in the hands of governments, and their instruments the teachers. What then would become of freedom?

I believe these fears are groundless.

First. There can be no escape from the national organization of education; the area of attack is too large, and the expense too great for the organization of national education to be left in the hands of voluntary bodies however heroic and public-spirited. And I do not see why the provision of the *facilities* for education should be left in the hands of voluntary societies. Apart from the evils of sectionalism and the growth of class education (as, for instance, separate schools and universities for the rich), the development of English education has been held back for several generations because we have allowed the provision of the *facilities* for public elementary education to remain in the hands of autonomous societies.

But in a national system of education the function of the state will be increasingly, as it now is partially, to provide the *facilities* for education conceived in the broad sense I have indicated. The state is bound to be authoritative in certain directions – to take a single instance – in many matters of conduct. But while we do not want the state to set itself up as an authority on certain other matters, of which I need not now speak, the state must and does act for the benefit of the community in the light of a minimum body of assumptions which are subscribed to with more or less degrees of acquiescence by all sections of society.

The state could provide the facilities for education in the broad sense

I have described, with the acquiescence of all parties in the state. And while the state would be neutral, as I think we should all want it to be, it would be providing the facilities for a full life for all its citizens. It would provide a theatre, so to speak, on which the lives of the citizens would be enacted; and such a life would be susceptible for a religious theory, metaphysical or positive. But the formulation of such views of life, philosophic and religious, will be and must be the duty not of the state but of autonomous societies within it. In the adult life of the community, much adult education will be and must be carried out by autonomous associations, which look to the state for means and facilities; and the same will apply to the numerous associations by which the social and recreative life of the community is nourished.

The whole welfare of communities and the vigour and prosperity of their intellectual and social life depends on the extent to which centres of unfettered initiative can be developed within them. In the state, frankly organizing itself as an educational institution, freedom and richness will be secured by the development within the state of large numbers of adult autonomous societies. They will be the guarantees for intellectual and spiritual freedom, the surest bulwark against the tyranny of the state in politics, industry, religion, science and art.

Second. I do not think we need have any fear of the wider scope and bigger office which the teacher would have when the life of the community is organized so that education is conterminous with life. For the office of teacher will be based partly on legal sanctions which can be appealed to in a court of law open to all citizens, and partly on rational sanctions which are positive and not transcendental (though, of course, I do not mean to say that transcendental sanctions are necessarily not rational). In the state system the effective sanctions governing the office of teacher cannot include sanctions which are valid only for a minority in the state. Nor will they be the sanctions of an organized professional class or clique; the teacher's office will base its claim to respect on grounds to which all men and women will be able to give their intellectual support, rational grounds common to all the sections of the community. And those sanctions will not be sacrosanct, because, while they will protect the office, they will not shelter the holder from criticism, and prevent him being dispossessed of his office. The unworthiness of the teacher will be held to hinder the effect of his office.

And we must not forget that in a community where education will be shared by all, where education will be the common process used by all in the effort to achieve a satisfactory and good life, and where the teacher, instead of being isolated in his classroom, freely mixes with other adult men and women in the general life of the community, the dividing line will be very thin indeed, and the difference will be rather one of degree than of function. It is only in a world where education is confined to infants and adolescents, and to the adult males of a favoured class that the teacher is liable to become a pundit or a tyrant.

There must be a large extensive development of the state system of education, so that it includes organic provision for every stage of adult life, and so that the centre of gravity will be in that part which provides for youth and maturity. We shall then achieve a system which educates those who control it.

Secondly, we should break down the didactic conception of education as having only to do with instruction and discourse, by associating the economic, political, recreative, and liberal side of adult life with education. We should then see education, not as a specialized process confined to one aspect of life, but as the process whereby the community organizes itself to secure for all its members the best kind of life in every direction. There would be no department of life in which the constructive energy of education would not be brought to bear. Indeed we should gradually reach a state in which the distinction between 'education' and every kind of constructive effort in the art of living would melt away.

We should therefore need to institutionalize education, and as a practical step towards this we should gradually reconstruct our buildings. In cities and towns this would take the form of connecting up all our schools, libraries and places of higher education, so that they would form an obvious unity, and effectively influence the recreative and liberal side of the community's life. In the countryside it will be easier still to link the life of the community in composite sets of buildings as we propose to do in Cambridgeshire.

In such buildings designed to shelter and nourish the corporate activities of our towns and the countryside, the art of English architecture should find its grand expression in this century.

It follows from such a synthesis that education would become not only the imparting of knowledge, but the induction into a way of life — education would be both science and religion.

It has been urged that the integration of the whole life of the community is a prime necessity if we are to avoid further loss and confusion and ruin. It has been urged that the function of the state in this effort of integration is not to set itself up as the sole guardian of the souls and bodies of men and women. As the state administers law, so it will furnish the facilities by which its citizens can achieve the highest life. The spiritual life of the community will be maintained and kept intact in the hands of autonomous associations; philosophy, religious systems, scientific discovery, intellectual freedom it will be their function to maintain.

They will be the guarantee of intellectual and religious freedom. We should picture the state providing, by the consent of all, those means without which men cannot begin to live a worthy life; as providing a threatre for the free and unfettered activities of its citizens; and side by side with the state large numbers of autonomous societies, such as educational associations like our W.E.A., religious societies and universities, upon which will lie the duty of nourishing the intellectual and social life of the nation.

I believe that it is on these lines that we shall be able to find the means for a renascence in the life of our country and at the same time retain our intellectual and political freedom.

3

A Modern Philosophy of Education

Introduction

Professor Thomson was professor of education at Durham University. He would have been surprised that this review of his book, which must have sadly disappointed and perhaps infuriated him, has survived more freshly and longer than the book itself. But it deserves to. The reason for its survival is that Morris used it as a means of putting over his own 'Modern Philosophy of Education', and in doing so he not only deprecated the feebleness of Professor Thomson's effort, but indicated his own philosophical position which was firmly in the rationalist camp.

He looks forward to the time when everyone will have accepted this position, for only then can we begin to articulate a modern philosophy of education, no longer 'thwarted by some otiose metaphysical reference'. Then, he suggests, 'education, both as a humanist philosophy and public policy, will become as exciting as war and perhaps...its moral equivalent'. He goes on to point out how education needs to be seen, not only 'as a matter of psychology but also as the essential part of social and political philosophy', a vision which clearly had not been grasped by Professor Thomson, whose book 'exhibits very plainly the chronic inability (with one or two exceptions) of the professional educationalists of the training colleges and training departments to make any contribution, either of originality or vigour, to contemporary thought on education'.

There are two points worth making in connection with the review. First Morris's use of the word 'racial'. In the twenties it had no connotations of ethnic differences, Morris was using it, as he uses the word 'race' further on in the paragraph, to indicate that the problem concerned the whole human race.

The second point to be made is that in turning his back on a transcendental view of life, he by no means dismissed the importance for humanity of experiencing what he liked to call a sense of 'the numinous', a sense of awe induced by silent meditation, by music, by poetry, and by the contemplation of the arts.

A Modern Philosophy of Education

Book review published in the
'Nation and Athenaeum' 25 August 1929

'A Modern Philosophy of Education'
by G. H. Thomson, Allen and Unwin

There is one condition on which the contemporary discussion of education can become scientific, logical, lucid, and relevant at all points to human problems. It is that we should expel from the sphere of discourse all concepts that derive from the magical view of man and the universe. There seems to be hardly a single aspect of education, either theoretic or practical, the consideration of which is not confused by the intrusion of the concepts of transcendentalism, hardly a problem the solution of which is not being thwarted by some otiose metaphysical reference. This is the case not only in Europe and 'America – where the dominant transcendentalism consists of Catholicism and its Protestant variation – but also in the East. Until we have the courage to proceed undeviatingly from the point of view of a rationalist positivism, the articulation of a modern philosophy of education is impossible. And this is true also of the development of education as a practical racial [sic] policy. The objectives of education, not as a mere matter of schools or the instrument of the sects, but as the principle of social organisation and welfare, cannot begin to be intelligently conceived, unless we decide, for instance, that the theistic cosmology of Catholicism is true or not true. Man, the immortal spirit, for whom his terrestrial career is a parenthesis, and whose instrument is not science but sacraments; and man, the mortal denizen of one of the humblest of the planets, who must fend for himself by the use of his own brains, and science and art, if the life of his species is not to fail – these two conceptions lead to mutually exclusive systems of values, incompatible in temper and irreconcilable in method. It is because the modern world is lodged irresolutely in the impasse created by these opposing views of man and his destiny, that educational philosophy and practice does not emerge into determinateness and most of the sayings of professors of education are confused and idle sayings. We must sooner or later decide between the two. The majority of educated people under forty know well which view must inevitably prevail. And when the scientific realist outlook becomes dominant, then education, both as humanist philosophy and public policy will become as exciting as war, and, perhaps, in the form of a planetary campaign, its moral equivalent. That we hesitate to make the choice in so far as it affects public policy is, in the opinion of many, involving the race in a dangerous loss of valuable time. There is one crumb of comfort, which is that modern progressive communities are finding it a matter of political necessity to model their common system of education on a non-'religious' basis.

Professor Thomson does not take a line; he refers to the impasse in a vague, unsuspecting sentence or two, and passes inconclusively on. It is not surprising, therefore, that, bereft of an unambiguous major premiss, he cannot see the wood for the trees, and that the book is a rather unilluminating discussion of secondary issues. He says nothing, beyond a sentence, of education as sociology. Reading this book you would hardly realise that in this century the most fruitful and far-reaching development of education is likely to come as a result of conceiving of it not only as a matter of psychology, but also as the essential part of social and political philosophy, and of regarding education as the fundamental principle and educational institutions as the essential material of concrete social organisation. You would not be reminded that the integration of modern communities, in all places and at all stages of culture, is likely to come about by organising them around their educational institutions. Education thus conceived will not be the entity adumbrated in training colleges, but the application, as a maximum measure, of science and art to the life of the individual and society.

It will be seen that the exciting title of this book is not borne out by its contents. The book discusses, frequently with an exasperating tentativeness that simulates scientific restraint, various stock problems of educational science and technique. It summarises, without any fruitful criticism, current educational policy. It exhibits very plainly the chronic inability (with one or two exceptions) of the professional educationalists of the training colleges and training departments to make any contribution, either of originality or vigour, to contemporary thought on education.

4

Rural Civilisation

Introduction

'Meantime, Bottisham Village College will be finished in January, Linton will be finished in March. I shall feel then with four V.C.'s the idea is permanently safe. I gave a paper on the subject at the September meeting of the British Association at Blackpool and went off the deep end.'

(From a letter to his friend Charles Fenn, December 1936.)

Here is that paper. But it is much more than an orgasmic high dive. Morris used the occasion to describe in detail the institution he felt was needed to rescue the English village from cultural, social and economic decay. Typically he begins by setting the scene, first in the context of history and then in the contemporary countryside, at the time beset with poverty and threatened with blight. (He took care to warn his audience against the all too common romantic attitude of the townsman, who is blind to reality.)

His solution lay in the development of the rural region, a grouping of villages around their nearest country town, where facilities for recreation, education and a diversity of opportunities for social intercourse could be as well-developed as in the city. They would be centred in and around the newly established senior school (which was the short-lived but important predecessor of the secondary modern school).

In his description of the necessary parts that together would go to form the whole building in which such facilities would be housed, he does not content himself with a mere list or even with a bare description. He often adds an explanation as to why a particular part is necessary. This he does with more than half an eye on the potential architect, reminding him of details that might otherwise be forgotten, and giving in each case the reasons for them. This attention to details, and his readiness to explain why they are necessary, was typical of Morris, the creative administrator.

He ends by sketching a wider and more distant horizon, forcing us (and his audience) to think historically as well as socially; to think especially of the threat of 'aimless leisure' and of his solution: 'We must sublimate with infinite resource, or fail.'

Rural Civilisation

Address to the British Association at Blackpool,
13 September 1936

I 'Each age is a dream that is dying and one that is coming to birth.' The English village as a social unit is a relic of the middle ages and the pre-industrial age of the seventeenth and eighteenth centuries. It belongs to a time when there were no roads in the modern sense and no rapid transport, and when, from the point of view of industry and social services, it did not matter whether people lived in groups of two hundred, five hundred or a thousand. The economical provision of social services and amenities demands a social unit of many thousands; and this is the reason why not only the instrumental services, such as sanitation, water and light, but also the immense development of education, especially of the secondary and technical type during the nineteenth century has taken place wholly in the towns of England. During the past thirty years, and even today, the countryside, if it desires educational opportunity, must seek it in the town. Since the industrial age began over a hundred years ago the countryside, not only culturally and socially, but in economic opportunity, has been increasingly dependent on our urban civilisation. Modern motor transport, rapid cheap and ubiquitous, is finally completing the process, so that the rural community of all ages, and especially the young, have their faces turned habitually to the town.

I suggest that we should be more realistic and less romantic about the village. The village has ceased to be an independent social unit. It has its own psychological limitations:

> Below me, there, stands a village and looks how quiet and small
> And yet bubbles over like a city with gossip, scandal and spite,
> And Jack on his ale house bench has as many lies as a Czar

The history of civilisation, it has been said, is the history of progressive towns dragging in their wake a reluctant countryside. The village looked at from the Tudor manor house or the Queen Anne rectory or the weekend cottage has quite a different aspect from that of the village worker and youth. By itself the independent village cannot provide the fuller life both culturally and socially that increased leisure and facilities make possible and which the young are determined to have. One of the most disastrous of our social failures is the omission,

48

in spite of our enormous wealth, to provide on a wide and imaginative scale communal facilities for every kind of cultural and recreational pursuit. Our towns are squalid and chaotic dormitories sicklied o'er with commercialised amusement; they should be deliberately organised by the community for the art of living the full life. Is it possible for the countryside to realise this ideal independently of the towns? That is the problem. The independent village has gone for ever. The only alternative to the complete subordination of the countryside to the town is the adoption of the rural region as a cultural and social unit, parallel to that of the town. The choice is no longer between village and town but between the rural region and the town. Unless we can interpose the rural region between the village and the town, the village is doomed and the victory of the town will be complete. I commend this to the consideration of those who imagine that they will preserve the village by resisting reorganisation in rural education.

The modern transport that will otherwise transform our countryside into a vast and far-spread suburb can here be our friend – it can make the rural region compact and accessible from all points, and can weld it into a genuine social unity. Indeed, one type of rural region, namely the small country town of two or three thousand people and its adjacent villages, already exists as a traditional and geographical unit in the English countryside – transport will serve to reinforce it. The other kind of rural region, a group of villages centering round a large village can, I suggest, be made into a no less successful cultural and social unit.

The Hadow Report has been published for just over ten years; and educationists and administrators and the public are just becoming accustomed to the idea of senior schools in central places for the education of the older children of the countryside. For many years I have personally urged the need for providing the countryside with something much more comprehensive – that is, not only with a post-primary system for the older children but also for the fullest opportunities for adult education including the countryside's own technical education in agriculture, and for recreation; that is, that there should be a cultural and social life for the countryside in its own right and independent of that of the towns.

To achieve this the rural senior school as such in its strictly conventional conception, with limited buildings and accommodation, and with its peculiar adolescent ethos, is insufficient; it may, in actual fact, prove an obstacle, organise it as a night school as much as we may. We must start with the conception of a community centre serving the population of a rural region at all points and at all ages – a community centre on as generous a scale as possible which, while housing the senior school in the day time, will provide a theatre for the habituation of the adult community beyond the school leaving age in Science and the Humanities and in Health and the corporate life. We have been hearing much during the past two years about the development of technical and adult education and of physical training and health education. We cannot provide technical institutes for small country towns, much less for groups of villages. The only way by which technical and adult education can be shared by the country towns and villages of England is by means of the community centre which houses the senior school in the day time. Here we have a solution that is as economical as it is effective.

By means of such a rural community centre I claim that the wide provisions of the Education Act of 1921, as they affect not only the school but higher and technical education, could be expressed with striking significance in terms of the life and industry of the countryside.

II I turn to the physical embodiment of the rural community centre of the countryside, that is to its buildings. Parenthetically, I should like to express the wish that we would allow our young architects to design our new schools. The architectural intelligence of England for all practical purposes is not allowed to make its contribution to the design of the buildings for public education owing to the system of official architects. As a result we have the provincial pseudo-architecture of the county councils and the municipalities, most of it a sight to put all heaven in a rage. In continental countries the best of living architects have been employed, and with their achievements in school design and decoration as well as functional fitness we cannot begin to compare. The cultural loss in England is beyond statement. It is just dawning on us that if we wish the young to appreciate Art we should first have educational buildings which are works of art.

The main limb of our community centre will be a large hall with a modern stage and cinema equipment, usually of not less than 2,800 square feet, such as the Board of Education have sanctioned in Cambridgeshire; attached to the hall there will be a good kitchen. In our rural region this hall will, in size, amenity and conveniences, be easily the best hall for public purposes – for drama, music, the cinema, dances, meetings and festivals. The uses to be made of it by the senior school are clear – assembly, midday meal, music, dancing, drama, speech days, and the rest. But the hall must be more than a school hall in size – if it is twice the usual size all the better.

The remaining accommodation of our country community centre will fall into four groups:

(1) A site of at least eight acres where the senior school has 240 pupils; better still twelve acres. There is a great need of spaciousness for our public buildings; and apart from the school garden, a rural community centre should have playing fields and a running track which will enable outdoor games throughout the year to form part of the recreational programme for the area.

(2) The classrooms for the use of the senior scholars in the day time, about which I need say nothing except that it is time we realised that the square or oblong is not the only possible shape for a classroom and that the circular classroom is at least as effective and is far more beautiful. In this connection I would stress the most imaginative use of colour in decoration.

(3) Rooms for practical activities. The minimum is a wood and metal workshop with the art room adjoining; a domestic science room and if a house is not available for the realistic acquirement of domestic crafts, a sitting room and a bedroom with a bath; a science laboratory and, if a separate engineering room is not to be had, an annex in which the internal combustion engine and electricity can be studied in their contemporary application to agriculture, industry and social life. Such a science laboratory should open straight out onto the school garden, or better still be placed in the centre of the school garden with which it may then form an experimental observational and teaching unity. Finally we should have a fully equipped gymnasium and at least an open-air swimming pool.

All these rooms for practical activities should be made large enough and be equipped for adult use in the evenings as well as for use in the daytime by the senior school. This is an essential requirement.

(4) The adult block.

First comes the library which will be the home of the county library and the school library – to be used by the senior school in the day time and by young people and adults in the evening. It will be a silent room with provision for reading and study.

Secondly, an adult lecture room of not less than 700 to 800 square feet, with a common-room adjoining, both of them sacred to adult use. These will be the focal point of adult education in the evenings and even in the day time. Here will meet university extension and other study groups; the debating society and union; committees of all kinds of local societies; the parish council of the central village. Round the walls cabinet lockers can be fixed and allotted to the main local societies for the storage of their documents and records. The common-room should have a hatch opening into it from the kitchen so that refreshments can be served, and there will be easy chairs and opportunity for silent games. The adult lecture room will be decorated and furnished so that it will look not like a classroom but a meeting place for young people and maturity – let us panel the walls with plywood which is as cheap almost as plaster and much more beautiful and serviceable, and provide semi-easy chairs and a few tables; never educational tables or desks.

I have stated what I regard as the minimum. I think there is a need for a games-room with a billiard table, table tennis and darts. A clubroom or hut for the very young people of 15 to 17 or 18 who have just left school is at least desirable, especially as a home for scouts and guides. Rural community centres should have a simple observatory, as accessible as for example the local inn, in which the country lad and girl and the older enthusiast can become universe-minded and acquire a valuable interest with as much naturalness as they learn to dance. Finally I would add a place for silence and meditation, of great architectural beauty. In it the senior school would assemble each day with the ritual of a corporate act accompanied by the hearing of the classic prose and poetry of the English Bible and by the great music of Europe. Our state educational institutions are classroom-ridden, lesson-ridden, textbook-ridden, given over to incessant didactic discourse and discursiveness. They lack ritual and rhythm and that kind of corporate ceremony in which the personality even of the young is freed and enhanced by the profoundly affecting dramatic combination of architecture, music, literature, and movement.

I cannot forbear to add that ideally the junior school of the central village or small town should form part of the community centre. Such a junior school, decorated and equipped with abandon and gaiety, should include a nursery classroom or rooms, a medical clinic and waiting rooms. Here would be the home of pre-natal and child welfare; of realistic child welfare instruction for the girls of the senior school; of the school medical service; of parental education and community education in health, especially by means of health clubs – in brief, a centre for the pursuit of health by education and preventive medicine.

Such a junior school would form a model on which the junior schools of the contributory villages would be formed; for I need not add that educationally the schools of all the villages forming the rural region should be regarded as an organic whole.

I hope I shall not be met with the prevaricating and frivolous query 'Can we afford all this?' Apart from the fact that our contemporary civilisation is a prodigal misuse and waste of human and economic resources and ignoring the blindness that does not see that health and education are the chief instruments of racial preservation, there is the new fact that social services and social reconstruction on a vast scale are the only ways in which we can hope to use the practically limitless increment of wealth that science and technology have potentially endowed us. We must rid ourselves of the infirmity of economy, and prepare ourselves boldly for an era, indefinitely long, of unremitting social reconstruction.

But much can even now be done within the four corners of the grant regulations of the Board of Education. The new building regulations disclose a remarkable advance, for in them the conception of the rural community centre, or indeed the village college with the rural senior school as its basis, is plainly set forth. Local education authorities are indeed invited to have this community ideal in their minds in designing rural senior schools. A commodious hall is rightly suggested as the first requisite; and then adequately large and equipped practical rooms, and a library. The suitability of the building and its amenities for evening use as a cultural and social centre are stressed. Though accommodation specially set aside for adult use is not mentioned, I do not doubt that the board would be prepared to recognise for grant an adult lecture room and common-room as they have done in connection with two village colleges now being completed in Cambridgeshire. To this extent, therefore, there is no financial obstacle to the realisation of the senior school as the community centre for the area it serves.

III Social progress is the substitution for one set of solved problems of a new and more significant set of problems making greater demands on human originality and energy. The solution of the economic disorder waits no longer on knowledge but on an effort of political will and administration. Already the new order of leisure is with us and has become, with an imperativeness difficult to express, the major problem of human society.

Neither in Europe nor America is there evidence of any community undertaking what is in our time, and will increasingly be, the task of the public authority – the provision of every facility that science and art can devise for the constructive use of leisure time. We need constantly to remind ourselves of the menace of aimless leisure amidst economic security, and that the decadence and disillusion that will arise with widespread intellectual and emotional unemployment will be more tragic than the sufferings of the long era of restriction and overworked poverty from which we are emerging. For the individual and for society it is the plain truth that, in the plenitude that lies before us, we must sublimate with infinite resource, or fail.

The grand task of education is frankly to convert society into a series of cultural communities. The most far-reaching development of education in this century will come of regarding it not only as a matter of psychology but also as the core of social and political philosophy so that education will be the fundamental principle and educational institutions the essential material of concrete social organisation. Our communities, whether urban or rural, must be organised around their educational institutions. Education corporately administered is the principle of unity by which modern communities can be significantly integrated at any stage of culture in East or West. Unity or universalism on the basis of any metaphysical belief is no longer possible in the modern world; and such beliefs must increasingly remain the province of the individual and of autonomous associations within the community. Education as humanist philosophy and public policy, as the application at a maximum measure of science and art to the life of the individual and society, may well become as exciting as competition and war and, in the form ultimately of a planetary campaign, their social and racial equivalent.

The next great phase of social constructiveness may be near; if so, we may then hope that our towns may be reformed and indeed rebuilt. I venture to suggest that the proposals I have discussed in this brief paper might make it possible for us to preserve, for some time, side by side with urban civilisation, a form of rural society, expressed in terms of the rural region, which will have a peculiar value in our own and indeed in every country in the world.

5
Post-War Policy in Education
Introduction

It was more than a year since Dunkirk, and the war had not gone well. However, already at home people were thinking seriously of 'post-war reconstruction', especially in the fields of social reform. The mass evacuation of school children from the city slums to the country had opened the eyes of the nation to the need for reforming action after the war. That operation, efficiently managed by the various local education authorities, had given them a justifiable sense of pride. This paper reflects that sense.

However, it is doubtful whether before or since there has ever been a serious suggestion put to the Association which was at once so self-assured (some would say arrogant) and so visionary. What makes it remarkable is not just the radical policies which Morris called upon his colleagues to promote, but the presumption that the Association should compose and publish a report on post-war policy which was openly intended to 'create public opinion'. His aim was that the report would make a real and lasting impact; to this end he goes into prescriptive details as to the style, format, print-run and price of the publication.

Sadly, but inevitably, his colleagues, without vetoing his ideas, did produce an anodyne and utterly unimpressive little pamphlet in April 1942 called *The Orange Book*. It caused as much stir as a pin dropped into a lake. An excerpt from a letter written in 1971 to me from Sir Graham Savage (who was Chief Education Officer of the London County Council at the time of the publication of *The Orange Book*) gives a hint of the reason for his colleagues' lack of enthusiasm: 'I should rather doubt if Henry Morris' ideas were incorporated at all in *The Orange Book*. He was usually so extravagant in his fantasies that both matter and style would need toning down if it was hoped that the matter would carry weight. He could never get off his hobby horse and he rode it to death...'

Here then are these imaginative and far seeing post-war proposals. Reading them now they could hardly be compared with a dead hobby horse.

His first major suggestions as to policy, namely the organising of communities around educational institutions and the massive expansion and extension of adult education, are repetitions of what he had written years before. They will be familiar to those who have already read the paper from the *New Ideals Quarterly* and his book review in the *Nation and Athenaeum* (pages 35 and 45).

He then stresses the need for a common system of state education and calls for the disappearance of the public schools which are 'based on the plutocratic principle'. Next he attacks the content of the curriculum in the post-primary school, and quotes whole passages from the Board of Education's *Handbook of Suggestions for Teachers*, where the expectations to be assumed of the average child are so unrealistic as to be funny. In doing this he proves his point that, when adult education is fully developed, such attempts to cram children at an early age (he termed it the pedagogic fallacy) will become unnecessary. Then it will be possible to free the schools from 'incessant didactic discourse' and open them up to 'aesthetic experience'. Deploring the obsession with 'knowledge' and 'information' he calls T. S. Eliot to his aid, quoting from 'The Rock':

> 'Where is the wisdom we have lost in knowledge?
> Where is the knowledge we have lost in information?'

He assumes the need for day continuation schools and does not forget the importance of reforming teacher training which at the time was utterly inadequate. He therefore makes useful suggestions for improvements in the education of teachers which would seek, not to increase their store of knowledge, but to contribute to 'their cultural sustenance'. He touches on the past failures of the Art Schools and on the unwillingness of public bodies to employ able young architects to design public buildings. He foresees the end of the 11 plus examination and calls on his colleagues to examine the existing system of public examinations and devise an alternative system. He makes three final suggestions. Let us substitute for 'state education' the more meaningful name: 'community education'. Let us replace the phrase 'equality of opportunity' with an alternative: 'equality of consideration'. Let us call for a Royal Commission on Education to be set up.

If *The Orange Book* had included one of his suggestions it might have made some impact.

Post-War Policy in Education

Paper read to his colleagues in the Association of
Directors and Secretaries for Education, 31 July 1941

The need for a comprehensive statement by the
Association on national educational policy

We are 'standing upon the forehead of the age to come'. A quarter of a century has elapsed since the last reshaping of education. Another and greater opportunity is in our hands. Moreover we now know better what we want, and we have a new public opinion consisting of more educated young men and women between 20 and 40 (the crop of the secondary schools and the technical schools).

I suggest that the officers of local education authorities should make a major and independent contribution to the elaboration of the educational system that will serve England for the second half of the twentieth century. We ought not, I submit, to be content to be dragged at the heels of the Board of Education as mere accessories, and for very good solid reasons. The board is a government body which cannot go beyond the limits laid down by a minister responsible to the Cabinet, itself responsible to a many-minded parliament. The education officers *as a body* are not constitutionally conditioned in this way. Speaking as a body they can express views of policy such as could not be expected of an individual officer, and they have more freedom than the board. In this circumstance alone the Association is in a powerful position both strategically and tactically.

The Association, reflecting the experience and thought of local government in education, can take the decisive and original lead in educational policy. If it does so nothing will more effectively justify local government in education.

I suggest that we should produce, not a memorandum, but a comprehensive report on post-war policy, which on the one hand would adequately express our point of view and on the other could be circulated throughout the country far and wide with the intention of informing, and indeed creating, public opinion – in the House of Commons, amongst teachers, in all the professions, amongst leaders of commerce, skilled workers, etc., etc. Such a document would have to be written not in the administrative English of memoranda but in literary and idiomatic English. I should hope that such a report might make thoroughly good reading; it could be well printed with the format of a Penguin special – and indeed must be printed at the price of sixpence and circulated by the ten thousand. A publishing firm could be got to take over such a project. A document meant both for experts and for laymen inevitably would have in part to deal with detail which concerned the former and not the latter. This need not cause any concern. The device of printing in smaller type sections which could be skipped by the layman without affecting the argument would for the most part meet the difficulty. And there is the device of appendices. We ought not, I suggest, to hesitate about going to the public. We have been able in the past at least to get an educational policy; we have failed in not getting the backing of public opinion.

I feel compelled to reassert that if we are to do this we shall have to engage expert subordinate secretarial assistance to enable the Association and its officers to get their policy into form. A single editing mind is essential if a report based upon dozens of sources and contributions is to be an organic unity in content and style.

The time factor arises. It should be possible at a fairly early date to arrive at a summary of headings of the policy, brief but detailed enough to enable the Association, *knowing its own mind*, to negotiate with the board or any other body about *their* proposals. But I would strongly suggest that we should reserve ourselves and issue our report as early as may be.

The fundamental principle of community planning is cultural

By necessity we are committed to a degree of community planning or replanning to an extent never known in our previous history. I use the phrase '*community* planning' of set purpose as inclusive of town planning and country planning and of *all* aspects of planning, and not only those envisaged by architects and town planners.

The first proposition which should be laid down by educationalists is that the fundamental principle and the final object of all future community planning, whether urban or rural, is cultural. This proposition will require much explanation mainly because it is new to town and country planners. Planning, even at its best, is universally conceived of in terms of the reorganisation of the economic and instrumental services of community life – industry, transport, housing, sanitation, water, light and amenities. We have to convince the new planning ministry and the architects that planning must provide not only for the economic and instrumental order, but also for the cultural and social life of the community conceived in its widest sense. Briefly, the cultural objects are health, education from the nursery stage to 18, adult education, social and physical recreation in community centres, and the consumption and practice of all the arts by the adult community.

If I may quote what I have already written:

The most fruitful and far-reaching development of education in our generation will come as a result of conceiving of it not only as a matter of psychology but also as the core of social and political philosophy; and of regarding education as the fundamental principle, and educational institutions as the essential material of concrete social organisation...

The organisation of communities around their educational institutions is capable of universal application in any society and at any stage of culture. It

58

is also the ultimate form of social organisation. It is the only method of escape from that impasse of modern society, in which some unity of communal life is necessary, but in which, by the operation of freedom of thought, a multiplicity of autonomous associations has grown up side by side with the state and replaced a single dominant view of life. A pluralistic society has taken the place of a monistic society, and architecture, both in the invisible hierarchy of values, and in the visual order of our environment, is difficult or impossible to achieve...

Some method for the integration of the life of the community with vital relevance to modern conditions is the prime social necessity of our time. The unity of social and spiritual life with its institutional and civic expression in architecture and organisation which was characteristic of the medieval town and the parish church and manor of the countryside has gone for good and all. But the effect, in modern times, of pluralism of associations and beliefs has been one of social disintegration, less evident in the village than in the contemporary town with its social fissiparousness and resultant architectural chaos. Since the breakdown of Catholic civilisation we have, so far as the social expression of values in communal living is concerned, been living on credit, consisting of the legacies of the forms of the Middle Ages and of the brief and brilliant, but morally impossible, eighteenth century.

Today we have to find a principle of integration which will allow unity of communal life and architectural expression and at the same time give free development to that pluralism of associations on which growth and freedom depend. In medieval Europe a common organisation for communal living was made possible by a system of common values and beliefs. In our time that element of unity in the life of society which is essential will be attained by the organisation of communities around their educational institutions. It is by some such synthesis that modern communities can again become significantly organic, that the decay of civic life and architecture can be arrested, and the planning of modern towns on lines of imaginative significance surpassing the achievements of the past, be made possible.[1]

The supreme need for adult education

I suggest that the development of a ubiquitous and fully-articulated system of adult education in its widest sense should be regarded as the most important part of reconstruction after the war. Such an extension of adult education would include activities at a number of levels, intellectual, social and recreative, with extensive provision for corporate life. The effect would be that the centre of gravity in the education

[1] Address: 'Institutionalism and Freedom in Education', New Ideals in Education Conference, Oxford, 1925; Lectures: 'Education and the Community', Cambridge University.

of a local community would not be in the school as it is now but in that part that provides for youth and maturity. Every local community would become an educational society.

When I speak of this extension of education, I do not mean merely the extension of formal education by instruction and discourse. I am thinking of the effective organisation of communal living and of the application at a maximum measure of science and art to the life of society. But we are so ridden by departmental views of education, so prone to look upon education either as a parenthesis in the human adventure or as a specialised process applicable to one or two aspects of life, that in thinking of education we think only of the school...I am using education to refer to the attempt by the local community, which is a microcosm and not a group of persons selected by reference to a particular age and class and sex, to achieve for all the highest sum of good life in every direction. That conception takes us a long way from the academic conception of education given by discourse in the class and lecture room.

If we regard education broadly as the process by which the community achieves for all its members the highest sum of good life in every direction as we are bound when we come to examine the structure and scope of public education – we shall rid ourselves of many false doctrines. We must beware of thinking of education too much in terms of the school; the tendency is difficult to resist because in practice the centre of gravity in public education has been the school. There, inevitably, the process, in so far as it is capable of autonomy, is, at best, a tentative organisation at an evanescent and feeble level of realism (the world of infancy, puberty and adolescence, in which neither ethics, nor law, nor philosophy, nor creativeness, with any absolute value, is possible) – in so far as it can take on a forward-looking relevance (towards the world of maturity in which day by day every man and woman, with remorseless necessity, must evaluate the intrinsic worth of life) one of preparation and preventive medicine. This latter aspect of the process has, as its main difficulty, the task of mediating the experience of maturity to the minds of the young for whom three-fourths of reality does not exist. Thus the problems of education during the period of creation after adolescence, and up to the stage of adolescence when creation that has any absolute value is impossible, are profoundly different...

When I say that the philosophy and practice of education needs a re-orientation of all its objectives from the point of view of adult welfare, I do not mean by this that the training of the young will become less important or that the study of the problems of the infant and adolescent in education can be relaxed. Of course not. But it is a fact, I think, that those engaged in the education of the young have seldom an adequate realisation of the ultimate scope of education. It is the intrinsic worth of the life that the adult leads, the working philosophy by which he lives, the politics of the community he serves in his maturity, the amount of efficient action he contributes to the community, that should be the main concern of education. That is why the centre of gravity in our system of public education should be in that part which provides for youth and maturity...

Those of you who have read the life of Sanderson of Oundle, will note how he was always stretching forward to the realisation of the school as a microcosm of actual life: 'schools', he said, 'should be miniature copies of the world'. What Sanderson wanted can never be achieved through the school alone, especially through a non-local school confined to one sex and one social class between the ages of 14 and 18. Sanderson's ideal can be realised in one way only, and that is within the actual local community through the instruments of education and local government. Under such conditions public education becomes the organised attempt of the local community to secure for all its members the best kind of life in all directions; there need be no department of life in which the constructive energy of education could not be brought to bear. Mark how the didactic conception of education as having to do mainly with instruction and discourse would gradually break down, so that by associating the economic, political, and recreative side of *adult* life with education, that word would receive a new content that would transform its significance. Mark too, that such an organisation of the life of the community would be brought about not by the fiat of a few officials, but by the community expressing itself through the instrument of self-government, so that in local communities education would not be merely a consequence of good government, but good government a consequence of education. What the State may be, what government actually is and its sphere, will increasingly be determined by the community organised educationally. The need is for educational institutions in which government and education are united as aspects of one activity. How much in this conception can those of us who are depressed and perplexed by the problems of democracy see possibilities of immense import! In the future our adult educational institutions will be the centres of determination, political, economic, social, and intellectual.

I am not, of course, pretending to give here even a sketch of the balanced exposition that would be given in our report. One or two further points may however be made.

(1) I should hope that we should all agree that it is in the development of adult education everywhere on the scale suggested that lies perhaps the main hope of finding some solution to the problems that beset humanity everywhere, especially of those problems which for their solution require the existence of an educated adult public opinion. Most of those problems form part of the sociological field. The universal sociological failure is the direct result of the non-existence of a complete system of adult education. It may take us fifty

years or even a century to get the system going. This need not dismay us. It has taken thirty years or so to get the secondary school system into working order.

(2) The local education authority, under the Education Act, 1921, including Section 86 as amended by the Physical Training and Recreation Act of 1937, has now full statutory powers to establish cultural institutions that are both centres of every form of adult education and community centres with every kind of social and recreational facility. What is required is that these powers should now be made duties, and that every urban and rural education authority should in consequence be obliged to draw up schemes for their areas.

I think that in this connection our report should indicate, if only briefly, the policies which are appropriate to urban and rural areas. In the city the technical institute or college can be the centre of all forms of adult education and the recreative centre of the city as well. It would have its full complement of social and recreative facilities, including common rooms, canteens, games rooms, etc. It would necessarily be supported in the wards or suburbs of a city by youth centres providing a balanced programme of education, social training and recreation. These would be accommodated in specially built youth centres or in senior schools with youth centres attached or in senior schools. These youth centres should be under the charge, not of head teachers of day schools, but of full-time trained supervisors or principals.

Another problem is that of the rural region consisting of the country town and surrounding area with a population of about four to ten thousand, of which there are hundreds of instances in England. What is to be their community centre? They are not large enough for technical institutes or colleges. How is the community centre for these small towns to be found – in buildings specially set apart for the purpose? In a community centre which accommodates the senior school in the daytime, but which has facilities and accommodation reserved for adult use? These questions require an answer and upon the answer depends the renascence of the country towns of England.

A common system of education

It is unthinkable that we should not place in the forefront of our report for the consideration both of the educational world and of the English people the case for a common system of education. It is not necessary in this memorandum to attempt to state that case, but there are some points in it which I should like to mention.

1 Part of the case, and the most profoundly important part of the case, against the public schools is moral. The English people, in the realm of the intellect, the spirit, and all the values – that realm in which, if anywhere, all members of the community, whatever their financial position, should find unity – has been driven into two nations not on any moral principle of division, based say on virtue and intelligence, but on a material principle based on money. It is impossible to compute the amount of intellectual and spiritual and moral damage that has been done and is still done by the system.

It is of course a universal tendency of human beings to significate and reinforce themselves by adopting forms of association, habits and practices, whose essence is that they are based upon a principle of exclusion. The evil of the principle is that it can only make a person feel superior in proportion as it makes another person feel inferior. But in civilised societies it should be one of the major objects of the educational system to counter this disruptive principle and to furnish children, men and women with positive and moral principles of signification. In England there is a disproportionate amount of social fear in all classes of society and everybody is hagridden by snobbery. Our condition is made more morbid than it need be by an exclusive system of education for a minority.

It should be stated without qualification and equivocation that (a) the basis of the public school system is financial, (b) that it is in demand not primarily because is cultivates intelligence and inculcates virtue, but primarily because it significates the individual on the basis of a principle of exclusion. Thousands of guileless boys are turned out to face the world with their self-confidence based not on the belief that men are members one of another, but on the consciousness of having attended exclusive schools open only to the children of parents above a certain income level.

We cannot prevent the continuance of schools based on the plutocratic principle, but we can at least expose their true nature in the hope that every gentleman and gentlewoman whatever their economic class will refuse their support and reinforce the demand for a common system of education so that the realm of values may also be the realm of social unity.

2 We ought to make it clear that there is no form of excellence in the public school, whether intellectual, physical or spiritual, that cannot be realised in a community school attended by members of all classes. We should also point out that the non-local character of the public

school, and its divorce from the local community, is a fundamental weakness. I should hope that we might be able to set out the possibility of boarding secondary schools which form part of the life of a city or country town. In such institutions there would be a combination of the advantages of a boarding school with accessability to the family, and to the life of a local community of which the school would form an organic part. In such circumstances a boy or girl's loyalty would be attached not to an exclusive non-local school, but to a local community. 'The theatre in which we express the greater part of our lives is a local theatre. While empires die at the centre nations wither at their extremities, and it is the quality of local life in a nation that matters in the end.'

3 As to the future there is the practical consideration that many so-called public schools are in receipt of public monies from local authorities and the board. I assume that we should unanimously agree (a) that all aided schools should form part of the public system of education and should not charge fees, and (b) that we should organise every possible kind of opposition open to us to any attempt to bolster up with public money public schools which continue to charge fees.

The content of post-primary education requires radical reform

A widespread system of adult education would enable us at long last to face up to the main fallacy of post-primary education. The characteristic fallacy of post-primary education everywhere in all countries is that to too great an extent it endeavours to educate the boy or girl at puberty or adolescence in terms of adult maturity. This applies to the conceptual sphere, to the factual sphere, and the sphere of all the arts: prose and poetry, music and the visual arts. The error is gigantic in its proportions and ill-effects, and is perhaps only to be equalled by the innocent unawareness with which it is persisted in by thousands of teachers as well as inspectors and examining bodies. We have by now learnt to devise the education of young children under five, from 5 to 7, and from 7 to 11 or so, in the terms appropriate to their actual psycho-physical stage, at the same time taking account of their instinctive inheritance and their inherited endowment. The decrease in child misery and increase in child happiness has been enormous. We have to do the same for post-primary education. We have, formidable as it may appear, to devise a system of post-primary education in terms of the psycho-physical stages, the instinctive inheritance and the varying inherited endowment of young people between the ages of 11 and so to 13, and 13 and so to 16, and to 18. We shall have by research to discover those art forms, whether of novel or story, of music or picture, which are appropriate to these ages, and contemporary artists must be asked to create new ones.

I am not here attempting a considered statement of the influence of what I propose to call the pedagogic fallacy, but there are some points that must be referred to.

For instance, in senior secondary and public schools Shakespeare's plays are introduced into the curriculum between the ages of 13 (sometimes under) to 16, and these plays include not only, for instance, *Midsummer Night's Dream*, but *King Lear* and *Macbeth*. Moreover children under 16 are made to 'study' *Paradise Lost* and Milton's shorter poems, and the poems of Wordsworth, Keats, Shelley and others contained in *The Golden Treasury*. The method of approach is almost wholly didactic. It is a process of unimaginative cruelty. The consciousness of the art of poetry is not shared by a large number of people; those that do are a very small minority of the adult population. Moreover, the consciousness of the art of poetry only occurs after the age of 16, even amongst the most sensitive, and then it is of the less subtle forms of poetry. The period of the deepening and development of the poetic taste is between 18 and 30. A contemporary poet and critic, Herbert Read, writes in his recent autobiography: 'It was not until my seventeenth year that I became conscious of the art of poetry. At school we read and even acted Shakespeare, and there were 'recitations' which must have included some prose, but I never read a volume of poems by choice.' Read goes on to tell how in fact he got this contagion later and then mainly through the influence of a literary tailor who befriended him. Read further remarks: 'The very abstractness of Shelley's poetry kept me at a distance. Shelley, I would now say, demands a degree of intellectual development which I did not reach by the age of 17 or 18. Tennyson was more open to my simple sensibility.' What applies to poetry applies also in the case of a great deal of the masterpieces of prose, including the Bible. The plain truth is that the supreme works of literary art spring from the complex experiences of the adult stage of men and women of genius, and we deceive ourselves if we expect undeveloped human beings at the stage of puberty or halfway through adolescence emotionally or intellectually to respond to *Lear* or *Macbeth* or *Ode on the intimations of immortality* or Keats' *Sonnets*.

Many boys and girls of 16 and onwards will not get on terms at that age with many of the supreme works of literary art. There is a chance that they may, but the time for the initiation of a young person to the arts is from 17 or 18 years of age onwards; and for the more extraverted and practical type it must be later still. Then we must also remember that many worthy members of society are not capable of ascending even to the middle levels of the arts. The pedagogic fallacy is committed not only in connection with the arts but also in the conceptual and factual side of education. Examples of the fallacy may be found in profusion in the Board of Education *Handbook of Suggestions for Teachers* published in 1937, two years eight months before the outbreak of the war. Throughout portions of that book dealing with the education of children in the senior stage there is, side by side with much that is enlightened, especially about the value and necessity of practical activities, a pervading assumption that the boys and girls under the age of 14 in the elementary schools can be taught in terms of the culture and concepts of adult maturity. Take, for instance, the section on History which is 33 pages in length. The authors say (page 413):

What may be achieved by the end of the (senior school) course —

When conditions are favourable, the child may perhaps be expected, by the time he leaves the elementary school, to have some idea of the stage in world history at which British history begins; of the peoples that were merged in the English nation; of the main social and economic changes through which the country has passed in the last thousand years; of the development of the national system of government; of the growth of the Empire; and of the present position of the British Commonwealth of Nations in the world. Above all, he should have begun to realise also that this story has some bearing on everyday life, and that the England of today and the British Commonwealth of Nations are the result of changes that can be traced through centuries.

With a touch of indulgence the authors add: 'This is the ideal, but it is recognised that to attain it fully may be beyond the reach of many schools.' Again (page 415):

The value of some background of world history —

Whatever the topics selected for inclusion in the Senior School course, it is desirable that the teacher should so present them that his pupils can see them against a background of world history. Thus, the story of our kith and kin beyond the seas, of their settlements and struggles, of the great deeds they have accomplished, of the development of the lands in which they have settled, or which they have administered, should be presented as an important and integral part of the story of the British peoples as a whole. But even British history only becomes intelligible when the pupil realises its place in the story of the world. When dealing, therefore, with the history of the British Dominions and Colonies, the teacher will have abundant opportunity to bring home to his class the fact that they cannot learn British history without learning it as part of a larger whole, and that their sympathy and respect are due to other nations and races, with whom whether as allies or rivals, fellow-colonists, rulers or traders, Englishmen have had, and still have, so many dealings. A respect for other civilisations than that of Western Europe will best grow out of a knowledge, however small, of their history. Even to hear once that the Chinese were a cultured people when our ancestors were savages may exercise a lasting effect on the outlook of a child.

Again page 416: *British History as part of World History: Some ways of dealing with Ancient History* –

No course of history can be satisfactory that leaves the pupil with the impression that the story of the world began with Julius Caesar's visits to Britain... The important thing in such teaching is to concentrate on those parts of the world's story from which modern civilisation can trace a direct descent, i.e. Palestine, Greece and Rome; it is easy to waste time on stories of primitive man or to devote too much attention to stories of the Asiatic Empires and Egypt. But, through Ancient History rightly taught in biography and story and picture, the pupil may learn to recognise what we owe to Greece and Rome: the feeling for beauty and the beginnings of scientific thought and method, on the one hand, the spread of law and order, on the other; and how the fusion of the two made western civilisation, as we know it, possible. Again, he may be shown how, as the Middle Ages drew to their close, renewed interest in the ancient Greeks and Romans altered the outlook of all western peoples, and how the university and the printing press passed on the inheritance.

Again on page 417 some hints are given for: *Linking up British history with world history* –

For example, if such topics as the following are dealt with boldly and simply the children may be expected to have a better understanding of our own history: Britain as a province of the Roman Empire; the raids and settlements of the Northmen; the Crusades, the Renaissance and the Reformation; the expansion of Europe overseas; the position of Spain under Philip II, of France under Louis XIV and Napoleon; the unification of Germany and Italy; the development of the United States of America; and the international growth of modern industry and commerce.

Then again on page 420: *The Middle Ages* –

In the treatment of the Middle Ages, outstanding features should be selected and illustrated by accounts of interesting and important personalities. Thus life in Norman times could be illustrated by William I and Henry II; the beginnings of Parliament by Simon de Montfort and Edward I; the story of Church by Hildebrand, Becket, St. Francis and Wycliffe; the wars of the Middle Ages, including the Crusades and ideals of chivalry, by Richard I and the Black Prince; the story of Wales and Scotland by Llewellyn, Wallace and Bruce; the growth of knowledge by Dante, Roger Bacon, Marco Polo, Prince Henry of Portugal, and Caxton; and the story of France by St. Louis, Edward III, Henry V and Joan of Arc. Such a selection of topics, if treated with proper attention to detail, would take up the time likely to be available for this period, and, with many classes, too great emphasis need not be laid on the thread of political continuity connecting them.

Without any attempt to define precisely such terms as feudalism, the gild, the Church or the manor, it will frequently be possible to bring home to the children's minds by concrete examples, how these characteristic institutions of the Middle Ages influenced the lives and actions of men of that day: what a prominent part, for example, the churchmen played in the making of history, how much power the ownership of land brought with it, and what life was like to the town dweller.

Again page 422: *The XVIIth Century* –

The constitutional struggle of the Seventeenth Century should be presented as simply as possible, and illustrated mainly by the careers of outstanding personalities like Hampden and Strafford...The beginnings of the British Empire in the Seventeenth and the first half of the Eighteenth Century – the story of the American Colonies, the early struggles of the East India Company, the settlements in Newfoundland and the capture of Jamaica – should receive due attention. Here the teacher will find great opportunities for an interesting treatment of Geography, for instance, by indicating the gradual penetration of the American continent from the French settlements in Canada and the English settlements in Virginia, Pennsylvania and New England, the Jesuit missionary stations on the Great Lakes, the explorations of La Salle and the founding of New Orleans, the line of frontier posts along the Alleghanies and the advance from West Virginia and Pennsylvania into Kentucky.

I forbear to quote more and will only say that the chapter on Geography, which is 35 pages long, is similar in character and these two chapters are part of a series of twelve chapters dealing with eleven subjects:

Health and Physical Training
Music
Art and Craft
Needlework
Housecraft
Gardening and other Rural Activities

English Language and Literature
History
Geography
Nature Study and Science
Mathematics

with an appendix thrown in on the League of Nations.

The assumption that the child between 11 and 14, or indeed 15, is intellectually, aesthetically and morally a grown-up person appears in many other sections of the Handbook, including those on English, Geography, Science, and the Arts, mixed up of course with much that is admirable. The same assumption pervades whole sections of other reports of the Board of Education and the Consultative Committee, for instance *Health Education, The Teaching of English in England*, the Hadow Report, the more recent Spens Report, and various specialist reports on secondary school curricula. The famous introduction to the Code of 1904 and used until 1926 and reproduced with admiring approval in the 'Handbook' of 1937 assumes indeed that children under 13 are not only grown-up, but are specially gifted with intellectual, moral and spiritual insight.

If this section of the report gets written it is to be hoped that the writer will examine the syllabuses of all the first and second school examinations held in this country. In them the pedagogic fallacy of projecting the intellectual and aesthetic understanding of maturity into the minds and personalities of young people under 16 and 18 is to be found complete. A critical treatise on them would clear away vast oppressive masses of human folly in English secondary education.

I have already hinted that when, in due course, we have a proper system of adult education we shall be in a position the more ruthlessly to relieve the post-primary schools of their burden of adult culture. Another reform will also be possible. Our state educational institutions, particularly the schools, are classroom-ridden, lesson-ridden, textbook-ridden, information-ridden, and given over to incessant didactic discourse and discursiveness. Even in the best schools, especially secondary schools, the element of discourse is overwhelming. The schools in future will include far more of the element of emotional training and aesthetic experience. The schools indeed should be the community centre for the consumption and concrete practice of the arts by children.

For those to whom this matter comes as new or who think the case overstated, I would quote the following from one of the greatest humanists of our time, who was also one of the gentlest and most deeply religious of men – Havelock Ellis:

There are many infuriating aspects to modern education. One such specially arouses my own fury. That is the widespread custom of introducing into the schoolroom, to be thumbed by innocent children, the sublimest works of human imagination. Little is thought of reducing to the level of mere schoolbooks Shakespeare and Marlowe and Milton, to sicken children (and teachers themselves often as innocently ignorant) who as yet can know nothing of the naked ecstasies and anguish which are here expressed and transformed in redeeming shapes of immortal beauty.

The Bible, for those who truly know it, is among such works of divine art, and it is the Bible, above all, which is thrust on to children who would find far more spiritual nourishment, if not in Hans Andersen's fairy tales, at all events in books of natural history such as K. de Schweintz's *How a Baby is Born.*

Where the superior officials are found who, against the judgment of many of the best teachers, ordain that children should acquire a life-long disgust for great literature and all that it can yield, I do not know. But until they are mercifully confined in homes for mental defectives the world is not likely to 'rediscover the Bible'.

Meanwhile the mind dwells on those Gadarene swine, possessed by devils, educational or other, which ran down a steep place into the sea and choked.

The Eagle soars in the summit of Heaven,
The Hunter with his dogs pursues his circuit.
O perpetual revolution of configured stars,
O perpetual recurrence of determined seasons,
O world of spring and autumn, birth and dying!
The endless cycle of idea and action,
Endless invention, endless experiment,
Brings knowledge of motion, but not of stillness;
Knowledge of speech, but not of silence;
Knowledge of words and ignorance of the Word.
All our knowledge brings us nearer to our ignorance,
All our ignorance beings us nearer to death...
Where is the Life we have lost in living?
Where is the wisdom we have lost in knowledge?
Where is the knowledge we have lost in information?

T. S. Eliot, from 'The Rock'.

The school leaving age

The school leaving age should be raised to 16 without exemption. We have been attempting to raise the school leaving age to 15 for about a decade and a half. If we are not now to envisage the raising of the school leaving age to 16 within a stated period, when are we to do so? To think in terms of raising the school leaving age to 15 only, introduces a factor of confusion into all our thoughts and planning about buildings, the curriculum, and staffing. We cannot hope during the decade after the war to organise at long last a complete system of post-primary education unless the school leaving age is raised to 16.

Day continuation schools and the period of 18 to 21

I am assuming agreement about the need at this stage for day continuation schools for the period of 16 to 18. I suggest that we should in addition discuss whether it is desirable or not to introduce an element of compulsion for some form of intellectual and physical training between the ages of 18 and 21.

The continued education of teachers

The correct diagnosis of some of the characteristic limitations of our English system of community education is that the main control, both locally and centrally is administrative and not cultural. Neither administrators nor administration (in which I include inspection) can create and inform true education; they can ensure formal efficiency (an important commodity, but achieved by ants and bees), but they cannot create and sustain authentic sanctions. It is not the task of administrators, as hewers of wood and drawers of water, whatever their private inspirations and dreams may be. The proper architects of education are philosophers, artists, scientists, prophets and scholars, operating in freedom.

The teachers, many after inadequate education and training, are sent to the schools and there they remain, many forgotten for years, some for a lifetime. Some, it is true, but too few, go to refresher courses once, twice or thrice in their careers. Some authorities have weekly courses on Saturday mornings. We have neglected to devise for the teachers a system for their cultural sustenance and continued training in the art of teaching throughout the whole of their working careers. From this point of view the system of inspection is of little or no value. The system of organisers for various subjects as it at present exists is often too casual and superficial.

It is a state of affairs for which we have got to find a remedy. For myself, I think that we have to examine the possibility of linking up all the schools in an area to the regional university and its education department. We could place the educational welfare of schools and the cultural and technical guidance of the teachers in the regional care of the universities of England and Wales, leaving the administration and administrative control in the hands of local and central authorities.

There would thus be two influences guiding the education system – on the one hand the administrative control of the local education authority and on the other the qualitative, intellectual and spiritual inspiration of the Universities effectively sustaining the cultural life of the teachers and reinforcing their capacity in the art of teaching. Under some such arrangement there would be constant traffic between the schools and the university and its departments. Teacher training would not end at 21 or 22; it would be regarded as a permanent process going on throughout the teacher's career.

We cannot allow the existing state of affairs to continue after the war. As a result of it no class is more intellectually leaderless than the teachers. We have somehow to find a method of ensuring that the education and technical training of teachers goes on throughout their careers.

Art and technology

The failure of the art schools to influence design, either amongst manufacturers and other makers of things on the one hand and on the other amongst the public as consumers, is plain for all to see in the contemporary bankruptcy of taste. Our report must deal with the lack in all classes of modern society of visual awareness, with the acceptance of ugliness, and with the failure of our academic art teaching. This is a large and stirring theme and there is much more to it than the complete collapse of the design of things in daily use. The restoration of the visual sense throughout society and the whole ordering of our external environment in terms of architectural art is a question not only of civilisation but of a sane and full life for everybody everywhere. With regard to the practical problem of bridging the gulf between the artists and designers and the industrial manufacturing world (which, with one or two exceptions, does not use the artist or the designer), we ought to study the only solution extant, so far as I know – that embodied in the Bauhaus at Weimar founded by Professor Gropius and described in *The New Architecture and the Bauhaus*, Faber and Faber, (trans. by P. Morton Shand), and in an article by Professor Gropius in *The Year Book of Education* (1936), 'Unity between Art and Technique as the Aim of Public Education in Art'.

Architecture

We have not made the advance that ought to have been made in the architectural character of our schools and in the design of their equipment. The main reason for this is that the architectural intelligence of England for all practical purposes is not allowed to make its contribution to the design of the buildings for public education owing to the system of official architects. In continental countries the best of living architects have been employed, and with their achievements in school design and decoration as well as functional fitness we cannot begin to compare. The cultural loss in England is beyond statement. If we wish the young to begin to appreciate form, colour and texture, then we must give them schools which are works of art. The holding of architectural competitions, both open and limited, and of the commissioning of able young architects ought to be a normal feature of policy in every city and county. There is furthermore a need for sustained research in the design of school equipment and furniture. This is a sphere in which our Association could on its own account take effective steps.

The common meal

There is a European precedent a thousand years old for making the common meal part of an education. The midday school meal as we know it is a travesty of this. We have been content to let it be a voluntary extra given free only to those children, who in various degrees, are starving. The time has come for making the common meal part of the life and training of the school, such as Scripture, English and Science, partaken of by every child and given without charge; and if administration requires it putting it formally on the timetable.

School examinations

The raising of the school leaving age to 16 and the development of a universal system of post-primary education will enable us in due course to get rid of the Special Place Examination at 11. I assume that we are all agreed about the necessity of introducing a system of psycho-physical records for all school children beginning in the infant school.

This leaves the problem of the first and second school examinations and all they involve in the secondary schools to be dealt with. I hope our report will include a brief examination of existing examinations and the layout of an alternative system.

Nomenclature

I venture to suggest:

(a) That it is more accurate to refer to 'community' education rather than to 'state' education. We want a phrase that does justice to the fact that public education is provided by elected local authorities and that the Board of Education is a partner in the matter.

(b) 'Equality of opportunity' is an unfortunate phrase and is said by some philosophers to be nonsense. One, Hastings Rashdall, in his book *The Theory of Good and Evil* suggests as an alternative 'Equality of consideration'.

A Royal Commission

The association should consider whether it should not press for the appointment of a Royal Commission on Education. The field to be surveyed is vast. The Consultative Committee of the Board of Education is considered by many to be a most unsatisfactory and inadequate instrument, and there is also widespread disagreement with a large part of the last report of that committee. There may be very decisive reasons against the appointment of a Royal Commission; if so we ought to hear them.

6
The Post-Primary Curriculum
Introduction

Although *The Orange Book* had appeared and he must have recognised that his own ideas for it had been totally disregarded, he returned to the attack with this paper on the curriculum. This can be seen as a more considered appendix to the paragraphs on the same subject which he had written for his colleagues in the previous paper (page 56).

This is a much more concise statement on a single theme, and is therefore probably more effective than the previous paper as a plea for reform. Certainly the ideas were taken up and in some respects implemented in the post-war period. He emphasised once more the need to remove from a curriculum designed for adolescents all that which, in all honesty, can be apprehended only by those who have had experience of adult life and reached maturity. He foresaw that the raising of the age of compulsory schooling from 14 to 16 would require an entirely new approach, providing for young people 'opportunities for new kinds of actions and pursuits that cannot be carried on in classrooms', and stressing the importance of the 'practice and consumption of the arts for feeling and enjoyment'. Such recommendations were made with pupils of all abilities in mind, but he conceded that for 'the able minority' special provision would have to be made, especially through a great extension of the libraries available to school students.

The Post-Primary Curriculum

Paper submitted to the Association of Directors and Secretaries for Education, 30 May 1942

1 It is generally agreed that the grammar school curriculum, although it has problems of its own, should not be considered entirely apart from the post-primary curriculum as a whole. The reform of the latter seems to me to be the most pressing item on the educational agenda. The giving of full-time schooling to the adolescent population of the whole nation raises grave problems of training and technique that cannot be solved by reference to existing orthodoxy.

2 Since we are planning to give full-time schooling to all children between the ages of 11–16, we shall be wise, in discussing curriculum, to make a distinction between the needs of children up to 16 and those between 16 and 18, especially as the latter are going on to full-time higher or professional education. I am setting aside for the moment such connections as exist between the curriculum under 16 and from 16–18.

3 A searching review of the post-primary curriculum is necessary, not only in the interests of the secondary schools, but because, as a number of very intelligent and important critics think, school teaching as at present envisaged and school teachers as at present trained have very little to give the majority of boys and girls between the ages of 14–16. The secondary school has an objective, but it is one predominantly created by examinations. Nobody knows what the senior or modern school is after, what it proposes to do if it can have its pupils to 15 or 16. The province has simply not yet been mapped out and when it is we shall have to train the teachers. In this connection we must realise that we shall get very little help from the Board's *Suggestions for Teachers* (1937). Of that portion of the book dealing with the senior stage a large part is, to speak frankly, ludicrous. Yet the weight of customary thinking is so great that chapter 5 of the Spens Report, in mentioning the 1937 edition of the 'Suggestions', refers to 'its enlightened analysis of the aims and problems of the modern school' which 'is a challenge to the grammar schools to take stock of their position which cannot be ignored'.

4 We are thus forced to ascertain more precisely what are the actual psycho-physical needs and capacities of adolescents, and in doing so we shall have to remember that the majority are active, practical types, many of whom will not be capable of going on to any advanced form of abstract, intellectual work, and a fifth to a fourth of whom are said to be dull and backward.

We shall find that post-primary education, and grammar school education in particular, attempt, with grievous results, to educate adolescents in terms of what belongs wholly to the experience and culture of maturity. This applies to the conceptual, factual and aesthetic spheres and to the sphere of morality and religion.

A radical re-orientation of the content and method of post-primary education is therefore required, not only for the benefit of the grammar school, but to ensure that full-time schooling for everybody up to the age of 16 shall not prove a gigantic disappointment and failure. Furthermore, we have to provide for the adolescent, opportunities for new kinds of action and pursuits that cannot be carried on in classrooms.

5 A disabling weakness of the post-primary school is its isolation and its divorce from the real world of *action*. It is precisely this world of action with which the children in later adolescence are striving to make acquaintance. We have to discover the contemporary equivalent to that element of reality which was provided by the apprenticeship system. This has a tremendous bearing on the post-primary curriculum.

6 There is another element which is utterly neglected in the schools, or perverted by the examination system, and yet it is an element which will do as much as anything to give reality to adolescent education. I mean the pursuit and consumption of art forms without any regard to examinations or of edification in the academic sense, and as opposed to the predominant tendency of education by discourse. I suggest that we can bring a big element of reality into all adolescent education to the age of 16 (and beyond), if the actual practice and consumption of the arts for feeling and enjoyment (playing and singing music, drama, dancing, painting, reading, reciting) form part of the daily life of the school. They should be practised as often as games, and consumed primarily for feeling and enjoyment and, like games, not for didactic analysis or examinations. Regarded in this light the arts can give actions of reality which will have a profound effect on the emotional balance and morals of adolescents. But I must add a warning that we must not make the mistake of using art forms which are only appropriate to maturity (e.g. tragedy and opera). There is a substantial body of art forms in prose, poetry, drama and music appropriate to adolescence, but it has not been systematically isolated and collected for ready use and reference. In the visual arts, such as painting, much less is appropriate. (The truth is that we need a big increase at the hands of artists of art forms of all kinds appropriate to the adolescent stage; it is one of the greatest needs of world civilisation.)

7 I venture to give a brief summary of propositions which I suggest are bound to form the prolegomena to any future curriculum for adolescents to the age of 16. I submit that the Association must make up its mind on these preliminary but fundamental theses, if a really critical and constructive contribution is to be made to the Norwood Committee's report.

A fundamental distinction must be made in the post-primary curriculum between the needs of those under 16 and those over 16 on the ground that for the younger group the training must be given predominantly in terms of adolescent capacity and comprehension, whereas for the older group the training can begin to be given predominantly in terms of the experience and culture of maturity.

A reform based upon this distinction involves radical changes in the post-primary curriculum under 16, consisting broadly in:

(a) the removal from the curriculum of what clearly belongs to the experience and comprehension of maturity – factual, conceptual, aesthetic and moral;

(b) the introduction of realistic activities not involving discourse or classroom technique, and having in mind the needs both of the able minority, the pragmatic and practical average, and the 'dull and backward',

(c) the ethos of the post-primary school is that of a group insulated from the surrounding world of action and reality. Unless this divorce can be got over the desirability of full-time schooling for all adolescents everywhere will be questioned or denied even in liberal and enlightened quarters, and

(d) the introduction into the life of all post-primary schools of the practice and consumption of art forms (singing and playing music, dancing, drama, literature, poetry and painting) for enjoyment and recreation, with as much freedom from discourse and examination as games. The schools should become community centres for the initiation of adolescents into art forms as a necessity for an adequate life, like the skills, religion, food and exercise.

8 It is not necessary at this stage to say much about the post-primary curriculum for the years 16 and upwards. In the grammar school it will clearly provide for that able minority which will be trained to take the intellectual lead in the universities, professions, administration, etc. It is during this period in the grammar school (as it will be in the part-time day continuation school) that the growing child can be initiated, with varying speeds and varying degrees of success, into the world of adult experience and creation.

It would be agreed that many children of the able minority will begin that initiation under the age of 16, but not many in any explicit sense; and such children can generally look after themselves and have every chance of getting all the help they need if, as will normally happen, they are recognised by their teachers in the grammar school.

But all schools, through their libraries, must increasingly provide for the service of access. In the library, double or treble its conventional size, all children should be able to approach the written word and the illustrated world at their peculiar level. For the abler children this is doubly important, since they will be able to do what is done by the child in the lucky home – take down the *Republic*, or Dante, or Eddington, or *Tom Jones*, or Botticelli, or Hogarth, etc. at the age of 14 and make an acquaintance with a whole nominal cosmos, which will fall into relevance later. But the point is that they will do this spontaneously and of their own free will.

7
Adult Education
Introduction

Morris admits on the first page of this article, in a footnote, that he has lifted much of it from the talk he gave to the New Ideals Conference a version of which was published in their journal in 1926 (see page 35) and also from two lectures he had previously given at the Cambridge Education Department, which have not survived. Their loss may not be serious, since it is quite likely that whatever, in this article, is not contained in the 'New Ideals' talk, will have been taken from the lectures. The editor of the present collection makes no apology for the repetitions, they serve only to emphasise the points Morris was making over the years.

As was usual with him, he begins by setting the scene, and insists that the centre of gravity in the public system of education needs to be shifted from childhood to youth and maturity.

He puts his faith in planning, but planning with a much wider brief than is normally accepted by planning departments, for he insists that planners must seek to provide not only for the material health and convenience of communities, but also for their social and cultural well-being. The aim should be to encourage a purposeful self-governing community. He admits that the complex nature of society today makes it more difficult to devise a cohesive community than in the past when the Church set common standards and established agreed patterns of behaviour. He painted a grim picture of contemporary society, especially of the modern city, but he saw in 'a fully articulated system of adult education' (which would include wide ranging activities – aesthetic, intellectual and recreative) a kind of lodestone which would draw the community together through its 'extensive provision for corporate life'. In this way a local community would be self-governed and because the community had, through education, become responsible, good government would become the consequence of education.

He sets out the legislative and administrative tasks facing the country if this ideal is to be achieved. He is prepared to be patient – 'such a system may take us fifty years or a century to get going, but that need not dismay us'. But for the ideal to be achieved we must retain intact the existing system of local government – that 'cornerstone of freedom as every dictator realizes when, on getting into power, he abolishes it'.

79

Adult Education

Chapter in the 'Education Handbook' (Ed.
E. W. Woodhead) Norwich, Jarrolds, 1943

Up to the middle of the nineteenth century only the governing minorities of societies were literate. Then began the process of making everybody literate. The process is hastening and it is reasonable to guess that by the end of this century men and women everywhere (excepting the mentally defective) will be able to read and write. Furthermore, the increase of wealth and leisure will by then have even more vastly developed. Parallel with these processes there has been a marked decay in the sanctions especially the religious sanctions, which formerly governed life. Our species, in solving the problem of poverty and overwork is in fact moving forward to a more difficult and perilous stage in its history. For what is called social progress, we have now learned, is not a movement towards a static perfection; it is the exchanging of one set of solved problems for a new and more significant set of problems making greater demands on human originality and energy. The solution of the economic problem awaits no longer so much on knowledge as on an effort of political will and administration. Universal comfort, with wealth and repletion and with large margins of free time, is the next great problem of *homo sapiens*. The human house will indeed be swept and garnished for a fresh fate. Words cannot do justice to the urgency and the wisdom of thinking out now new institutions to enable communities to face this new situation. To do this we must arm ourselves with two conceptions which are, in fact, complementary: First, adult education (in a wide sense which will be described later) is the major part of education. The centre of gravity in the public system of education should reside in that part which provides for youth and maturity. Second, the fundamental principle and the final object of all future community planning everywhere, whether urban or rural, must be cultural.

Community planning

I take the second proposition first. Planning, even at its best, is universally conceived of in terms mainly of the reorganization of the economic and instrumental services of community life – industry, transport, housing, sanitation, water, light, and amenities. We have to convince the new Planning Ministry and the architects in our own country that planning must provide, not only for the economic and instrumental order, but also for the cultural and social life of the community conceived in its widest sense. Apart from the programme of the schools up to the age of eighteen, those cultural objects are religion, the practice of mental and physical health, adult education, science and the humanities, social and physical recreation in community centres, and the consumption and practice of all the arts by adults whether in groups or individually.

The most fruitful and far-reaching development of education in our generation will come as a result of conceiving of it not only as a matter of psychology but also as the core of social and political philosophy; and of regarding education as the fundamental principle, and educational institutions as the essential material of concrete social organization.... The organization of communities around their educational institutions is capable of universal application in any society and at any stage of culture. It is also the ultimate form of social organization. It is the only method of escape from the impasse of modern society, in which some unity of communal life is necessary, but in which, by the operation of freedom of thought, a multiplicity of autonomous associations has grown up side by side with the State and replaced a single dominant view of life. A pluralistic society has taken the place of a monistic society, and architecture, both in the invisible hierarchy of values, and in the visual order of our environment, is difficult or impossible to achieve... Some method for the integration of the life of the community with vital relevance to modern conditions is the prime social necessity of our time. The unity of social and spiritual life with its institutional and civic expression in architecture and organization which was characteristic of the medieval town and the parish church and manor of the countryside has gone for good and all. But the effect, in modern times, of pluralism of associations and beliefs has been one of social disintegration, less evident in the village than in the contemporary town with its social fissiparousness and resultant architectural chaos. Since the breakdown of the Catholic civilization we have, so far as the social expression of values in communal living is concerned, been living on credit, consisting of the legacies of the forms of the Middle Ages and of the brief and brilliant, but morally impossible, eighteenth century. Today we have to find a principle of integration which will allow unity of communal life and architectural expression and at the same time give free development to that pluralism of associations on which growth and freedom depend. In medieval Europe a common organization for communal living was made possible by a system of common values and beliefs. In our time that element of unity in the life of society which is essential will be attained by the organization of communities around their educational institutions. It is by some such synthesis that modern communities can again become significantly organic, that the decay of civic life and architecture can be arrested, and the planning of modern towns on lines of imaginative significance surpassing the achievements of the past, be made possible.

The scope and objects of community planning have not been thoroughly thought out, much less reduced to systematic form. It is one of the great needs of civilization. The truth is that in Europe since the disintegration of the medieval economy of town and country, in the setting up of colonial communities in new lands, in the vast spaces of the East during modern times, no systematic attention has been given through science, art, and administration to the planning of man's environment to meet his social and cultural needs. Everywhere, in this and all countries, the town has failed, or is beginning to fail, to be an effective instrument of community life. The objects of the town, both as an environment and as the instrument of a way of life have to be thought out afresh. Otherwise further decadence stares us in the face.

When this war is over we must not repeat the incredible mistakes that took place in the 21 years (1918–39) that elapsed between the two wars.

A few simple statistics give us some measure of the magnitude of those mistakes. During the 21 years 550 municipal housing estates, each of over 500 dwellings, were put up serving a population of 2,750,000 in Great Britain. In only 85 of these housing estates was any attempt made to provide community facilities, and these consisted of wooden huts, converted houses, and, in some cases, halls. Only about 13 of these 85 centres could be considered reasonably adequate and nearly half of them were provided, not by the statutory authority, but by voluntary bodies.

In the same period there were established 82 municipal housing estates, each of over 1,500 dwellings, in England and Wales, serving a population of 1,000,000. Here again community facilities were provided on only 36 estates, and these consisted of huts, converted houses, or adapted schools.

In the housing estates put up by private enterprise the situation was even worse. It is estimated that on such estates, serving a population of 1,500,000, only about 100,000 people had community facilities of any kind provided for them.

The future in adult education

A cultural breakdown has taken place in the towns and cities of England, and it is not absent from the countryside. As has already been said, it is partly due to the decay of religious sanctions and it is aggravated by the increase of leisure. Some signs of it are to be seen in the addiction, terrifying in its proportions, to commercialized amusements, football pools, dog racing, watching professional sport with all the accompanying betting, to the passive pursuit by day and night of the films and the wireless, to cheap newspapers and, in recent times, to astrology. Other aspects of it are the great aimless crowds in the streets and the public-houses at weekends; the acceptance as normal by the greater part of society of the hideous squalor of our towns; and the many thousands who live in the long streets put up by the speculative builder, who have no centre of signification and seem to be known only to the rent-collector and the undertaker. Finally, there is the epic dullness and malaise of some hundred of industrial and country towns with no corporate tradition of cultural activity and amenity.

The development, therefore, everywhere and for everybody, of a fully articulated system of adult education is the most important of all the tasks that lie before us. Such a development of adult education would include activities at a number of levels, intellectual, aesthetic, and recreative, with extensive provision for corporate life. The effect would be that the centre of gravity in the education of a local community would not be in the school, as it is now, but in that part which provides for youth and maturity. Every local community would become an educational society.

When I speak of this extension of education, I do not mean merely the extension of formal education by instruction and discourse. I am also thinking of the effective organization of communal living and of the application at a maximum measure of science and art to the life of society. But we are so ridden by departmental views of education, so prone to look upon education either as a parenthesis in the human adventure or as a specialized process applicable to one or two aspects of life, that in thinking of education we think only of the school.... I am using Education to refer to the attempt by the local community, which is a microcosm and not a group of persons selected by reference to a particular age and class and sex, to achieve for all the highest sum of good life in every direction. That conception takes us a long way from the academic conception of education given by discourse in the class and lecture room. If we regard education broadly as the process by which the community achieves for all its members the highest sum of good life in every direction as we are bound to do when we come to examine the structure and scope of public education – we shall rid ourselves of many false doctrines. We must beware of thinking of education too much in terms of the school; the tendency is difficult to resist because in practice the centre of gravity in public education has been the school. There, inevitably, the process, in so far as it is capable of autonomy, is at best a tentative organization at an evanescent and feeble level of realism (the world of infancy, puberty, and adolescence, in which neither ethics, nor law, nor philosophy, nor creativeness, with any absolute value, is possible) – in so far as it can take on a forward-looking relevance (towards the world of maturity in which day by day every man and woman, with remorseless necessity, must evaluate the intrinsic worth of life) is one of preparation and preventive medicine. This latter aspect of the process has, as its main difficulty, the task of mediating the experience of maturity to the minds of the young for whom three-fourths of reality does not exist. Thus the problems of education during the period of creation after adolescence, and up to the stage of adolescence when creation that has any absolute value is impossible, are profoundly different.... During the stage of infancy and early youth teaching is bound to be divorced from serious creation; in maturity teaching separated from creation is vain. In much adult education the separation between teaching and creation tends to persist, largely because as I think the problems and methods of the schools have occupied most of our attention. When I say that the philosophy and practice of education needs a re-orientation of all its objectives from the point of view of adult welfare, I do not mean by this that the training of the young will become less important or that the study of the problems of the infant and adolescent in education can be relaxed. Of course not. But it is a fact, I think, that those engaged in the education of the young have seldom an adequate realization of the ultimate scope of education. It is the intrinsic worth of the life that the adult leads, the working philosophy by which he lives, the politics of the community he serves in his maturity, the amount of efficient action he contributes to the community, that should be the main concern of education. That is why the centre of gravity in our system of public education should be in that part which provides for youth and maturity.... Those who have read the life of Sanderson of Oundle, will note how he was always stretching forward to the realization of the school as a microcosm of actual life: schools, he said, should be miniature copies of the world. What Sanderson wanted can never be achieved through the school alone, especially through a non-local school confined to one sex and one social class between the ages of 14 and 18. Sanderson's ideal can be realized in one way only, and that is within the actual local community through the instruments of education and local government. Under such conditions, public education becomes the organized attempt of the local community to secure for all its members the best kind of life in all directions; there need be no department of life in which the constructive energy of education could not be brought to bear. Mark how the didactic conception of education as having to do mainly with instruction and discourse would gradually break down, so that by associating the economic, political, and recreative side of *adult* life with education, that word would receive a new content that would transform its significance. Mark too, that such an organization of the life of the community would be brought about not by the administrative fiat of a few officials but by the community expressing itself through the instrument of self-government, so that in local communities education would not be merely a consequence of good government, but good government a consequence of education. What the state may be, what government actually is and its sphere, will increasingly be determined by the community organized educationally. The need is for educational institutions in which government and education are united as aspects of one activity. How much in this conception can those of us who are depressed and perplexed by the problems of democracy see possibilities of immense import! In the future our adult educational institutions will be the centres of determination, political, economic, social, and intellectual.

It is in the development of adult education on the scale suggested that lies perhaps the main hope of finding some solution to the problems which beset humanity everywhere, especially of those social and political problems which for their solution require the existence of an educated adult public opinion. Such a system may take us fifty years or a century to get going, but that need not dismay us. It has taken us forty years to found our secondary schools.

Next steps

The first step is *legislative*. Every authority for higher education, under the Education Act 1921, including Section 86 as amended by the Physical Training and Recreation Act of 1937, has now full statutory powers to establish cultural institutions that are both centres of every form of adult education and community centres with every kind of social and recreational facility. What is required is that these powers should now be made duties, and that every urban and rural education authority for higher education should, in consequence, be obliged to draw up schemes for their areas and submit them to the Board of Education. This is plainly necessary if, as a nation, we are to get anything done during the fifty years following this war.

Furthermore, the legislation dealing with housing and town planning should make it incumbent on all planning and housing authorities to consult the local education authorities so that proper provision can be made, not only for schools, but for all forms of adult education and recreation.

The second step is the *administrative* task of thinking out the various forms of organization and their physical accommodation. I have no doubt that for the villages and country towns (numbering something like four hundred) of rural England the solution will take the form of community and adult education centres which house the senior or multi-lateral school in the daytime. That covers at least a third of the population of England, and from the point of view of quality a precious part, and perhaps the heart, of England. But, according to the Scott Report, 'more than one-third of the population of England and Wales lives in the six largest city groups of "conurbations" of Greater London, Birmingham, Manchester, Liverpool, Leeds–Bradford, and Tyneside, and over half lives in or near the 14 chief urban centres.' We await the Government's method of dealing with this problem of congestion. The further overcrowding of urban areas is unthinkable. What we require is a policy of decentralization and dispersal, both of industries and population, from such areas, and if that is done then community planning with a cultural objective requires the creation of a new type of town. The task awaits the creative genius.

But even in the built-up areas of our large cities, adult education is a service which can be developed almost indefinitely, using existing buildings, secondary, technical and the new 'young people's colleges', for accommodation. There still remain a large number of small towns with a population ranging between fifty thousand to about one hundred thousand where existing senior schools could be added to, and new senior schools consciously planned to serve for adult as well as school use.

Residential adult education

Adult education and corporate life in residential colleges can provide a valuable and perhaps an indispensable element in the culture of the community, but it cannot take the place of the reconstruction of the local environment of the community and the family. And that is the first item on our agenda, both in the order of thought and in the order of time. I would add to the need for residential colleges to which men and women may repair for periods of several months, the need for holiday settlements in which a holiday, at once civilized and exciting, can be spent. This is indeed a field which could best be taken over by an autonomous, cultural body – otherwise the field will be exploited, as is already partly the case, by agencies working for profit.

Freedom in adult education

In this country the autonomous association has been the foundation of our intellectual, religious, and political freedom. We tend to forget that local government is also a cornerstone of freedom, as every dictator realizes when, on getting into power, he abolishes it (Napoleon in France, Mussolini in Italy, Hitler in Germany). There can be no escape,

I think, from the provision by the community of the physical facilities for a public system of adult education, and not through the State, be it remembered, but by democratic elected local authorities. One can picture this provision of physical and financial facilities as existing side by side with a large number of independent voluntary organizations for cultural purposes, receiving public help on condition of reaching defined standards. This applies, not only to academic, but to artistic pursuits, especially drama, music, and the ballet, for, as Lord Keynes has remarked, a subsidized autonomous body may well do something important through inadvertence or daring that would be regarded as improper by a government department.

Further, the system of local government in education, essential and precious as it is, requires a supplement. The control of education, both locally and at the centre through the Board of Education, tends to be administrative rather than cultural. We should associate the universities of England with the service of adult education everywhere. Already the universities have developed an extra-mural function of this kind. Throughout its area the regional university, through joint *ad hoc* committees, should be organically associated with the local education authority in supervising the service of adult education.

8
The Village College
Introduction

This talk is a model of its kind, but a strangely dated model; the style of its exposition is seldom heard today on the radio. However it serves as a kind of monument to a moment; it is the reminder of a time when a new wine, in the form of a new approach to education, was being poured into new bottles, that is, into the newly formed village colleges. At the same time, the fact that the talk was put out to the Far East is a reminder that the idea of community education was and remains exportable. The interest of people from all over the world in the Cambridgeshire experiment became almost a nuisance in the county education offices, where the clerks, secretaries and advisors had to deal with a stream of foreign visitors, especially from the Commonwealth.

Having set the scene in the countryside where 'everything moves as in a perpetual dance', and having emphasised the importance of bringing civilisation and delight to those who live in the country, he pictures the senior school (which children between 11 and 14 attended) where the school has become a society with a way of life and where the school dinner, 'a scene of happiness, gaiety and health', has become a part of the curriculum. As an extension of this he shows young people and adults coming into this school, into a building designed for them as well as for their children. It all has the quality of a vision, but 'without vision the people perisheth', and as Morris said in another context, 'Education is wedded to the belief that the ideal and the actual can be made one.'

The Village College
Talk given on the BBC Far-Eastern Service, February 1944

Everywhere in the world, East and West, the life and outlook of the countryside are precious and must be preserved. The towns and cities have, of course, their essential part to play in civilisation, but there is something unique and indispensable which the countryside can contribute to the welfare of mankind. What is this? In part it consists of the nervous sanity and balance both of body and mind, which comes of a life lived in contact with the sights and sounds of nature – of animals, tame and wild, of birds and fishes, of tree, plant and flower and all growing things, of forest, mountain and stream, of the sky in sunshine and cloud and in starlight. In the city the environment of brick and stone is stock still; in the countryside everything moves as in a perpetual dance. The human stocks bred in the countryside are the roots of our race, physically and mentally. And yet, alas, all over the world there is something wrong in the countryside, so that everywhere we witness the drift from the countryside to the towns. The trouble is partly economic and I am not going to deal with that problem because it is not my job. Part of the trouble is lack of proper housing, water, heat and light. The countryman has as much right to these amenities as the townsman. But one of the biggest troubles of the countryside is the lack of a good education for the children and of a proper social life for the young people and the grown-ups. Increasingly, all over the world there is an increasing leisure, and increasingly there will be a profound need for worthy social and educational opportunities for the adult population. How is this to be done for the countryside, as it must be done in our day and generation? I believe there is an answer and it has been tried out to some extent in the county in which I live, Cambridgeshire, England.

Up to a short time ago every village in our country had its school ranging from anything from thirty to one hundred and fifty boys and girls from 5 to 14. As someone has said, the education given consisted a great deal of 'chalk and talk'. We found it necessary to plan schools for the older children of 11 and upwards in central places, either small country towns or large villages. These senior schools have marked a great advance because they have not only made possible better accommodation such as halls and workshops, but also specialist teachers and classes of boys and girls of the same age and something like the same standard of attainment. The secret of these senior schools is activity – the major road to knowledge both for children and grown-ups. Let me describe one of these senior schools.

Here the mechanical use of the text book and the piling up of parrot facts unrelated to the child's experience is finished. The school has become a society with a way of life. Every morning you would see the boys and girls coming from the various villages on foot, on bicycle, or 'bus, all of them full of zest. The morning assembly is a cheerful affair bright with music and hymn with the Bible lesson read by a pupil. Within a few minutes the senior school has become a hive of constructiveness. One group is in the six-acre garden with its adjacent laboratory and greenhouse. Here all kinds of vegetable and fruit are grown for experiment and demonstration. Seeds and manures are tested, pigs, poultry and bees are cared for and fed, accounts and records are carefully kept, flower gardens and lawns are beautifully tended. It is a school estate in which the simplest boy in due course can acquire for life an understanding of a fundamental scientific law that affects all living experience – the law of cause and effect. Other boys and girls are in the wood and metalwork shops, making real things for the house and garden, using what has been well called the 'thinking hand', and thus satisfying a manual instinct as old as the human race. Furthermore they learn the more surely how to measure, how to add, subtract and multiply, because all these mathematical operations are given meaning and reality. Again, in the rooms for cookery and housewifery and infant welfare, vital human needs and instincts are the medium of training. Note another point of interest: it is that History and Geography start out from the history and geography of the surrounding countryside – from its industries, its agriculture, its geological formation, its rivers, its plant life, its beasts, birds, moths and butterflies. Not only the mind but the emotions are catered for in the senior school, which becomes a community centre for the enjoyment of the Arts. These include dancing, music and the drama. At midday there is one of the most important events in the life of the school, the common meal at which boys and girls sit together. Tables are charmingly set out, there is a fine sung grace and the children sit together with their teachers. Here is a scene of happiness, gaiety and health. The boy or girl who has sat through these common meals for four or five years will have acquired sound food habits for life and a fund of good manners. Finally, the senior school can make religion a thing of reality for the boy and girl in a way which cannot be done by preaching and exhortation. The senior school is a society in which the growing boy or girl have daily and hourly opportunities of *practising* in a way they understand what have been finely called the *actions* of religion, in particular co-operation, unselfishness, helpfulness, kindness, affection, trust. In the senior school, as elsewhere, religion is caught rather than taught.

Thus the senior school all over England is creating fresh opportunities for the boys and girls of 11 to 16 never before enjoyed in the countryside. But the school is not enough. Indeed a good deal, perhaps a major part, of what we have done in the school may be lost unless we do something more. We begin to enter more fully into the world of reality at the age of 16 and the golden time for education, especially self-education, which is the most real form of education, is between the ages of 16 and 30. In the countryside we need adult education. That is why the senior school and its counterpart everywhere should be made part of a community purpose and pattern. This is not an idle dream. In my own county of Cambridge we established before the war four community centres which serve a group of ten villages of a population of seven to ten thousand people. These centres, or village colleges, house in the daytime a senior school of the type I have described. In the evenings, at weekends and during holidays the village colleges are used by the grown-ups of all the surrounding villages, for education and recreation. How is this done? Certain rooms in the village college, such as those for cookery and housewifery, for woodwork and metalwork, for chemistry and physics, for art and engineering, etc., are equipped both for adolescents and grown-ups. All the classrooms have chairs and tables instead of desks and are designed from the outset for use by adults and children. The hall is rather larger than usual and is used as cinema, theatre, concert hall and dance hall. In addition, and this is very important, each village college has accommodation wholly set apart for the use of the young people and adults who have left school. At Impington, for instance, there is a common-room, a committee room, rooms for table tennis, billiards, etc., and a fine panelled lecture room with easy chairs. There is a good library for adults which also houses the books used by the children of the senior school. In addition, therefore, to serving students at evening courses, in arts, crafts, languages, history, drama, physical training, agriculture, etc., members of clubs and societies who use the common-room, canteen and library, and those who come to public functions such as dances, lectures, concerts, etc. Education is a continuous progress extending through childhood, youth and the whole of adult life. By housing organisations appropriate to all three stages in one building we hope the village college provides an easy passage from school to youth activities and from these to adult activities. We find that about two-thirds of the children leaving the senior school do in fact come back to the village college in the evenings. The youth work of the village college gains over that of the ordinary youth centre by the fact that young people are not segregated and that they can, and do, join in adult activities quite freely.

Other additions which we hope to make when the war is over are a swimming pool with physical training room adjacent; a dining hall, and a hostel for 50–100 beds. Residential courses, especially during weekends, are becoming a regular feature of adult education in the countryside. The work of the village college is not confined within its walls. The staff fosters the social life, education and the arts in the villages round about, though clearly the central institution can provide amenities and equipment which no single village could afford or maintain. The village college provides country people with something of the social life, the entertainments and the opportunities which the town offers, and it provides them in a rural environment, in a self-governing community of their fellows, and with a cultural background.

That blue-print is, I believe, valid for the countryside everywhere, both East and West, and at every stage of culture.

9

The Community Centre and the School in Rural and Urban Areas

Introduction

With the vast extension of adult education after the war, which Morris saw as being of the greatest importance, a problem would arise as to where it should take place. He himself had no doubts; secondary schools everywhere should be associated with the provision of community facilities for young people *and* adults; and by community facilities he meant places for both physical and intellectual exercise, for both physical and intellectual enjoyment. He lists these places giving details of dimensions and furnishings, and assumes that the Young People's College (a dream that died from cuts) would also be placed in the same centre or on the same site.

Cities presented certain difficulties, but he saw good reasons why even in the city every secondary school should be designed as a community school, open to adults as well as to children, while specialised educational functions for adults would be situated in a central college.

The Community Centre and the School in Rural and Urban Areas

Paper prepared for a meeting of the British Institute of Adult Education on the housing and accommodation of adult education, 28 April 1944

I take it that our discussions are proceeding on two assumptions:

(a) that adult education is at least as important as education for infancy and adolescence. My own opinion is that the centre of gravity in education and in the future will and should reside in that part which provides for youth and maturity;

(b) that adult education includes, not only intellectual training, but aesthetic (including the emotions) and social life.

I should like to add that we are discussing the problems of adult education with a third assumption in mind, that the future welfare of our country (and all countries) depends on the universal provision of adult education in its widest sense.

The development of adult education will require (i) teachers, instructors, leaders, etc., and (ii) accommodation. These notes deal only with accommodation.

Is there any possibility in the quarter-century after the war of providing accommodation for adult education on a wide scale in country or town? I think there is one hope and one only. It is that the provision of the secondary schools everywhere under the new bill should as far as possible be associated with the provision of community facilities for young people and grown-ups.

I Rural Areas

In the rural areas the application of such a plan is perhaps easier to envisage than in the towns. Either in a central village serving other villages, or in a country town serving itself and the surrounding villages, the new Modern School or Secondary School should be housed in a community building. Such a community building or buildings will house the modern school in the daytime; in the majority of places the Young People's Colleges; it will have certain accommodation that can be used by adults in the daytime; and the whole set-up will be available for young people and the adult community in the evenings, at weekends and during school holidays.

Where there is a senior school with an annual two-form entry (approximately 60 in the future) we should require a site of a minimum of 20–30 acres to provide for (i) the buildings, (ii) the school garden and estate, and (iii) playing fields for school children, young people and adults.

Accommodation for the modern school

Little need be said about this except that all the form rooms, especially the practical rooms, which will be used by the modern school, should be furnished and equipped so that they may be used for young people and adults. The conventional assembly hall, used for school gatherings, the drama, music, etc., must be avoided. Instead, there should be a theatre with a sloping floor for drama, music, the cinema and the dance. A large dining hall will provide the space necessary for functions such as dancing.

Accommodation set aside for adult use

The essentials are as follows:

A common-room furnished with easy chairs, tables, writing materials, etc., and with refreshments available. We have little experience about size, but my opinion is that such a common-room should not be less than 1,200 square feet.

One or more lecture rooms furnished with easy chairs and panelled, say, with plywood (which is cheap and avoids redecoration and is good to look at). These rooms are the places in which all kinds of adult education groups meet; minimum size 1,200 square feet.

Library. This should be the home of the school library, the county library and the stationary reference library. It should be as large as possible, minimum 1,000 square feet. Preferably, it should have attached to it a room for reading, with periodicals.

Committee room. A room of 300 square feet is invaluable for the constant meeting of the committees of all kinds of local bodies.

Games rooms. Table tennis, darts, billiards perhaps, a card room.

Accommodation for the Young People's College

I assume that the situation of the Young People's College should not be isolated, but should be in an environment which provides for young people *after* the age of 18. I realise that in certain places geographical conditions are such that attendance at the Young People's College will be seasonal and residential, and not once or twice a week. In the majority of places, however, geographical conditions will make weekly attendance possible; and in rural areas the small numbers will make it impracticable to provide a Young People's College in isolation.

Apart from the accommodation provided for the specific daily (and evening) use of young people, there should be some accommodation for their social life in the evening. The minimum is a girls' room, a boys' room and a common-room, with a small canteen. Young people of 15 to 18 or so must have a common-room and games rooms of their own.

II Urban areas

In a town of 60,000 and over it is impossible to centralise in one place adequate facilities for adult education and recreation for the whole community. The argument that I have applied to the modern school in the village group or the country town applies to the modern school which serves the ward or district of a town or city. In these wards community buildings housing modern schools in the daytime will provide for informal types of adult education and for recreation; the highest forms of systematic technical education are bound to be provided at the technical school or college.

I myself think that it will be proper to put the Young People's College on the same campus as the modern school and community centre. As I said above, we should proceed on the assumption that the Young People's Colleges must be situated in an environment which looks towards and provides for youth and maturity.

Finance

It is impossible to give details of finance but, on the basis of some experience, I think it may be said that if a modern school costs one pound it is possible to provide a community centre housing such a modern school for twenty-five shillings to twenty-seven shillings and sixpence.

The point is that by this method we provide a really adequate community centre and at the same time we make available for the adult community practically the whole of the 'set-up' of the modern school.

10

Community Centres

Introduction

This is yet another memorandum submitted to his colleagues in the Association of Directors and Secretaries for Education. Judging by their reaction to his suggestions for *The Orange Book*, they probably took little notice. It is however important as an indicator of his thinking on the contentious question of control. Under whose authority should the community centres operate?

Clearly there were disagreements as to how the community centres, now approved by government, should fit into the pattern of local amenities. He, predictably, was adamant that they should be firmly-rooted in existing educational institutions and administered through education authorities. He attacks somewhat virulently, the voluntary associations who would greatly prefer community centres to be separate both from schools and from the education authority. More than this, they wanted a free hand, or at least a major say, in running them. To the contention that centres should be democratically run, his response was this: 'I do not see much future for community centres divorced from the public system of education and run mainly out of public funds by self-elected associations.' And it is surely true today, that where community centres are not attached in some fairly binding way to a community school or college, they are usually under-used, under-staffed, and poorly-financed.

He is equally insistent that the County College (the Young People's College of the previous paper) should be connected to, and share facilities with, the secondary school and the associated youth club.

Finally he puts forward the idea that small villages, where there is no secondary school or college, should not be debarred from having a community centre of which the junior and nursery school would form one element, along with a hall, committee rooms, games rooms and a playing field serving both children and adults. At the same time he stressed the importance for two-way communication and co-operation to be active between these smaller centres and the larger central community college.

It is interesting to note that this pattern of community primary schools was pioneered by Cambridgeshire after Morris had ceased to be education officer, and has been taken up by most of the authorities which have adopted a bold policy of community education.

Community Centres

A note to the Association of Directors and
Secretaries for Education, January 1945

1 We should not allow ourselves to forget the vastness of the problems or the fact that between the two wars local education authorities were unaware of the problem and therefore did not begin to deal with it even though they had the powers (some explicit and others implicit). As so often happens when the statutory authority is asleep, a voluntary association attempts to appropriate the area of some social need. When, however, a short time ago the ministry set out to write a report on community centres it was found that neither the statutory authority nor the voluntary associations had much to show.

Here are some statistics for the period of 21 years (1918–39) between the two wars.

Municipal housing estates, all of over 5,000 dwellings and housing a population of 2,750,000, were established. Some 85 so-called community centres were set up, 49 of them by local authorities (mainly housing authorities) and all these were wooden huts or converted houses and only four were considered to be reasonably adequate. Some 36 centres were put up by voluntary bodies and of these, ten were wooden huts or converted houses, and only nine were considered reasonably adequate.

During the same period, 82 municipal housing estates of over 1,500 dwellings, providing for a population of 1,000,000, were established. 36 so-called community centres were set up, most of them wooden huts or old houses adapted, and out of the whole, only three were reasonably adequate.

During the same period, private housing estates were put up for 1,500,000 people, and only four so-called community centres were set up.

During the period referred to, very little or nothing was done in established urban areas, and practically nothing in the whole of the rural area of the country.

2 The Ministry's Report settles a fundamental issue. The local education authority is to have the major responsibility for the provision of community centres and of their maintenance apart from receipts. Doubtless the voluntary associations would have liked it otherwise.

They would even have preferred the housing authorities to the education authorities, but the logic of the situation could not be resisted. The statutory authority, of course, alone has financial resources to tackle what is after-all a universal public need. Moreover, the community centre ought not to be divorced from further education, the service of youth, the county college and the new secondary schools. I do not see much future for community centres divorced from the public system of education and run mainly out of public funds by self-elected associations. Nor do I think the housing committee an appropriate body. The powers of the Minister of Health with regard to community centres have been given over to the Minister of Education – it is a pity that locally the powers of the housing committee have not been similarly transferred to the Education Authority as was recommended by the A.D.S.

There are two important points to be borne in mind when dealing with the cant which is talked, especially by the voluntary associations, about freedom and democracy. The instrument of freedom in this country is and always has been the freedom to associate in defence of some intellectual, moral or social cause. The voluntary associations have confused this freedom with the claim that a public institution for the community is best administered by a self-appointed section of it. The other illusion is that local government is undemocratic and self-elected voluntary societies democratic.

3 I think we shall all be agreed that community centres should be given, both in the letter and in the spirit, the same kind of instruments of self-government as the secondary schools are. Moreover, it is necessary that the users should be actively associated with the management by appointing representatives on the managing bodies.

4 A word or two about the types of area:

Urban. There is no experience available showing decisively how the local education authority could best tackle the problem. There will have to be experiments. There is something to be said for putting the modern school, the county college and accommodation for grown-ups all on one site, and thus all three being used as the community centre for the ward or district. An alternative is that each ward or district should be served by a building consisting of the county college, the service of youth and the community centre. The main point here is that part-time education and recreation for young people of 16 to 18 should not be isolated but placed in a context looking forward towards maturity. As to the technical schools and colleges, there can be no doubt that they should be fully developed on their humane and recreative sides and that they will serve as community centres for their students, but I suggest that they are bound to be supplemented in each town by community centres for each ward or district.

Rural. Here we come to a region in which at almost every turn you are likely to meet some infuriated voluntary worker full of reasons why the local education authority cannot do the job. I suggest that in the larger part of England the rural region, consisting of a country town or a large village with the surrounding villages, provide the catchment area. There is no need to make the stupid assumption that everything will be done for the centre and nothing for the contributory villages. Each village must have its village hall linked up in all cases with the school. Indeed the contributory villages might well have their community centres consisting of the junior school with infant and nursery class, a hall with a committee and games rooms, infant welfare centre and playing field. Contributory villages should have their youth club and such evening classes as are possible. At the centre there will be provided those facilities which cannot be provided at individual villages (the logic that leads to the centrally-situated modern school applies with equal force to further education and community life. There must, however, be two-way service between the contributory villages and the centre. The only people who are interested in creating an opposition between the contributory villages and the centre are certain voluntary associations. By this time the opposition to community centres serving a rural area on grounds based upon the objection to 'going back to school' and to travelling should have been decently interred. In the countryside the objection to going back to school refers to the old full-range schools with one, two, three or more classrooms, not to the new senior schools and certainly not to any contemporary community centre housing a senior school. As to travel; everything, of course, depends upon the distance and the type of vehicle you have to travel by. But every night in the year is not wet and cold, and even now there are many young people in the villages in the countryside (and there will be many more after the war) who are happy to go much more than four to five miles for some activity or pursuit which they think worth while. In this connection it is futile to pretend that a village of 500 can offer the same facilities for further education and social life as a centre in a large village or country town.

I take the association of the community centre with the modern school in the countryside for granted. I do not see how it will otherwise be practicable to provide the facilities that are necessary. For myself

I hold there is positive advantage in putting the modern school, the county college and the community centre on one site. There is no need to be doctrinaire about the rural region. There are areas, doubtless, particularly in remote and hilly districts, where the centralisation I have referred to may not be practicable. On the other hand, the small country town, not only in the South but in the North, has been from the Middle Ages the traditional economic, social and religious centre of the tract of country surrounding it. The renascence of this ancient unit awaits a rebirth through education and the community centre.

11
Buildings for Further Education
Introduction

'We live without complaint in a wasteland of un-art'

To his rather drab title I have added a more telling sub-title taken from the talk which follows, since the talk at times reaches towards those almost poetic heights which he often touched on in conversation, and in particular when addressing architects. Here, for the audience of specialists, he brings together his feeling for history, his consistent concern for the arts and his undetachable interest in the salutary potential of education.

He compares the squalor of the contemporary city with the possibility then available of planning and building new towns which could become instruments 'of the truly civilised life'. He starts with the buildings necessary for education: the school, the college, the community centre. He emphasises the silent influence of well-designed and beautiful buildings upon those who use and pass through them, 'the eternal lesson of the Universities of Oxford and Cambridge'. To ensure high standards across the whole country he suggests the formation within the Ministry of Education of a special branch consisting of architects, designers and artists who would make themselves available to local authorities, not merely to advise on educational buildings, but on furniture, colour schemes and landscaping. This was a seminal suggestion because, only a few years later, the A. and B. Branch (the Architects and Buildings Branch) was set up within the ministry. It has had a benign influence on educational building ever since.

But his main aim, as he states at the end of his talk, was to explain to the architects the essential connection between the *buildings* for further education, and *his concept* of further education. His concept, as he briefly outlines it in this talk, is something which few people understood in 1945. There are still people in powerful positions both in education and in architects' offices who have not understood it yet.

Buildings for Further Education
An address to the Royal Institute of British Architects, 26 April 1945

The state of affairs is so parlous that I do not think it is possible to put with sufficient force the need of architecture in all places of education.

The age of industrialism and democracy has brought to an end most of the great cultural traditions of Europe, not least that of architecture. In the contemporary world, where the majority are half-educated, and many not even a quarter-educated, and where large fortunes and enormous power can be obtained by exploiting ignorance and appetite, we are in the presence of a vast cultural breakdown which stretches from America to Europe and from Europe to the East. It affects thought and speech, religion and art, and the increase of speed, comfort and convenience serves only to emphasise our lack of standards. Modern society is a body without logos.

Nowhere is this cultural breakdown more evident than in the collapse everywhere of our visual environment. For me the ordering of the whole of our visual environment is the major premise of architecture, and in architecture thus conceived I include not only the architect, the engineer and craftsman, but also the painter, the sculptor and the landscapist. Ugliness is one of our modern diseases. We live, without complaint, in a wasteland of un-art. The evil consequences, of course, are profound. Art, with architecture, is not the whole need of man, but with science and religion it forms part of the permanent three-fold need of our species. Much of the malaise of modern life is due to the lack of an environment ordered by the artist and the architect. There is consequent loss to every member of the community of balance, vitality and happiness.

Where are we to turn to counter this disease of squalor and ugliness? Elsewhere, and on many occasions, I have said that a revival of art and architecture, inconceivable in its scope and exceeding in its significance what has previously happened in history, will come about as a result of the reconstruction of our visual environment at the hands of the architect and the artist. It involves the reconception and rebuilding of the towns as the instrument of the truly civilised life. I cannot pursue that theme further. But I suggest that we can, at least, make a beginning with our schools, our places of further education, community centres – even with our art schools! The design, decoration and equipment of our places of education cannot be regarded as anything less than of first-rate importance – as equally important, indeed, as the teacher. There is no order of precedence – competent teachers and beautiful buildings are of equal importance and equally indispensable. To this proposition I would admit no qualification whatever. Human culture at its highest has always acted on this assumption; it is the eternal lesson of the Universities of Oxford and Cambridge. We shall not bring about any improvement in standards of taste by lectures and preachings;

habituation is the golden method, as old as Plato's *Republic*. Buildings that are well-designed and equipped and beautifully decorated will exercise their potent, but unspoken, influence on those who use them from day to day. This is true education. The school, the technical college, the community centre, which is not a work of architectural art is to that extent an educational failure.

Let us not deceive ourselves. What I have just said is not believed or appreciated by the majority or by more than a few teachers and administrators, or even architects. This act of recognition has somehow to be brought about, if possible before the great new programme of educational building is started on. The great professional organisations of teachers have done nothing to educate their members and should begin to make this omission good without delay. I remember that on an important government committee which was dealing with buildings, a teacher representing secondary schools remarked: 'Mr Chairman, I hope that no aesthetic consideration will stand in the way of school buildings being put up rapidly after the war is over.' Education officers, too, want educating in this matter. The last and most important problem is the architect. Here is where the failure fundamentally takes place. The architectural profession has wakened up too late, if in fact it *has* wakened up, to the importance of local government and to architecture both in housing, town planning and schools. I should like to have seen Sir Edwin Lutyens Architect for the County Council of Elysium in the South West and Mr Edward Holden Architect and Surveyor for the City of Athens in Lancashire. The system of official architects could be more successful than it is (Wren was an official architect), but it must be supplemented. At the present moment the largest part of the architectural intelligence of England is not able to make its contribution to education because of the somewhat rigid system of official architects. Some way must be found round this obstacle. During the next ten years an enormous programme of building for schools and colleges will be carried out. The architectural staffs of educational authorities will be hard-pressed. We want the help of the outside architects, not only because of the technical and artistic contribution they would make, but because of the sheer weight of the work to be done. This is a problem about which the R.I.B.A., all the teachers' associations and local government bodies should get together at once, under the aegis, perhaps, of the Ministry of Education.

I have been emphasising the place of school buildings as one of the most important parts of education, as the first instrument to hand whereby we could begin to habituate the community at all levels to a worthier standard of design and colour to the permanent benefit of our visual environment. Here is one of the most urgent problems of education. The time has surely come when the Minister of Education (who understands and is a friend of the Arts) should reconceive the function and scope of his architectural department. It should be made far more influential. It should be increased in numbers and reinforced by the recruitment of some of the best of our younger architects. First, the department, acting on the assumption that well-designed buildings and furniture and good interior decoration are a necessity and not merely desirable, should aim at nothing less than giving a definite and imaginative lead on the aesthetic aspects of all educational buildings. And this it should do with the avowed object of lifting the standard of taste of the whole community. At the present moment such a lead does not exist. I cannot go into details of how this lead should be given, except to say that, first, attention could be called to existing schools of architectural merit, and, secondly, the Ministry should boldly put out specimen plans and designs.

Do not let us be put off by suggestions that this programme would be expensive and what is called 'idealistic' and 'visionary'. It is imminently practicable and if expensive at all, only in the use of brains and imagination. We must underline what is a fact, that well-designed and beautiful school buildings can be built at a reasonable cost and probably less than depressing badly-designed and ugly buildings; and that gay and exhilarating colours do not cost more than county council brown or municipal green.

A second task is still to be done; it has to do with the technical aspect of school buildings and their efficiency as the working tool of education. It is the scientific and quantitative aspect of school buildings as distinguished from the qualitative and aesthetic aspect. It includes, on the one hand, materials, lighting (natural and artificial), orientation, heating, storage, corridors, equipment, types of tables, desks, seats, etc. etc.; on the other hand, the fundamental problem of the organisation of the school, that is the relationship of the various rooms, laboratories, workshops, quadrangles, three-sided courts, etc., to each other.

We sorely need an authentic corpus of sifted information and experience about the equipment and organisation of school buildings (as well as a bibliography of work that has already been done, as, for instance, by the Ministry of Works), having in mind, of course, the pupil and the experience of the teachers. There is no consideration arising in the life of the school which should be left out. Unless we get this we shall have numerous architects in different places working alone on the same problems, oblivious to certain needs and errors, unaware of solutions that others have found elsewhere. Such a body of doctrine and detail, which will be cumulative and will change from time to time, can only be brought together by the central Ministry working with some instrument of permanent consultation between teachers, inspectors, administrators, architects and manufacturers.

It is to be hoped these matters will be pursued outside this hall and up and down the country. To paraphrase the words of Shelley, what we want is the creative faculty to invest our knowledge with imagination and then the courage to embody our imagination in fact. As Bacon observed: 'Men, when a thing is to be done, ask why it should be done; when it has been done they ask why it was not sooner done.'

I turn to my specific theme, buildings for further education. The school is not enough. For over twenty years I have been saying that the centre of gravity in education should be in that part which provides for youth and maturity, and Sir Richard Livingstone has said much the same thing in a book published during this war. It is only by some such universal development of adult education that we can begin to tackle all the problems that beset us, and I mean by adult education something much more than education by discourse. I mean what Whitehead means, the pursuit of science, the practice of art and the life of religion. We have not used sufficient courage and imagination in working out the scope of adult education for modern democracy. We have suffered from a vocational education which has not been made the basis of a liberal education. We have not associated the aesthetic with technical education and have regarded them as two different worlds. The corporate and recreational have been left out. The one-sided idea of education for leisure has grown up. One of our deepest needs is somehow to significate the economic order and, social reform apart, I think that an essential step to take is to combine technical education with the community centre, and to provide in towns, and indeed the countryside, for the whole personalities of men and women. I would include in such places chapels for worship, silence and meditation, where the sense of the holy and the sacred can be nourished. As Whitehead says: 'The life of man is founded on technology, science, art and religion. All four are inter-connected and issue from his total mentality.' Thus, our community centres in town and countryside must be places that furnish a way of life. They should give significance and training for vocation and leisure, and provide both for the intellect and the emotions, for the personal and the corporate. It is a material vehicle for such a way of life that must be contrived by the architect: nothing less than this is needed.

I turn to two major aspects of further education, the urban and the rural. I shall not discuss residential non-local further education, for I put the locality first. It is the redemption of the locality which must be the first item on our agenda. It is in the locality that we spend our daily lives. In the blitzed areas which we shall reconstruct, and in the possible new towns, we should demonstrate that the ultimate object of all planning is cultural. Thus, the place of adult education, with its theatre, its library, its reading rooms, its laboratories, its debating hall, its common-rooms, may be made the focal point of the new towns. But even in existing cities we can do much. The technical college at the centre of a large town should include science, aesthetic and the corporate. An enterprising city would put its civic centre, its theatre, its concert hall and its adult college on one spacious site. There remain the suburbs; we cannot do everything at the centre. In each ward I should take the modern secondary school and make that and the part-time education of the 16–18 year-olds the nucleus of the community centre of the ward. There are positive advantages in doing so. The first is educational. Our schools tend to get isolated and insulated. No-one, I think, will propose to establish county colleges for a two-years range in isolation. For the school it will be a positive advantage; for the county college it will be a positive necessity that it should be placed in a context looking towards youth and maturity. Then, in the hard time ahead of us, when every unit of labour and when every ton of material will have to be considered, it will be the economical and, indeed, the only practicable way of getting community centres on any scale. It is better that the county colleges should serve districts of a city, with units that can be intimate, corporate wholes, rather than that a county college of thousands should be attached to the technical college. Thus, the community centre will house the modern school and the county college during the daytime, making available to children, youth and grown-ups in common, such things as halls, gymnasia, swimming pools, workshops, dining rooms, clinics and crèches. But, in addition, let each such centre have club rooms set aside for the evening use of young people of 15 to 19, and a wing sacred to grown-ups, consisting of a common-room, games room, committee room, lecture rooms, library and reading room. Let the lecture rooms be panelled with sycamore or walnut plywood and furnished with easy chairs. Thus, apart from the technical college at the centre of a town, every suburb or ward would have its community centre providing for the family group. We often hear of the modern equivalent of the village church as the centre of village life. Remember that the village church provided for the whole family from birth to old age; the community centre should aim at nothing less. The rejection of this point of view in the ministry's booklet on community centres is, in my opinion, a fundamental error. One technical point of great importance. The hall used for assembly, cinema, drama and dance, etc., should be replaced by a theatre or auditorium with a sloping floor which can be used for drama, music, ballet, cinema, large meetings and assemblies. In addition, we should have a hall for dining and dancing. The practice of the arts, both at school and in adult education, positively requires a theatre with a properly equipped stage.

Some such solution as I have described is possible in the villages and small towns of our countryside. Only by some such method can the life of the countryside be renewed, especially the life of the small country towns of England, which are almost wholly devoid of community facilities. The English country town of five to seven thousand with its surrounding villages is an ancient economic and social unit that has come down to us from the Middle Ages: it awaits a rebirth at our hands. In a typical town of the type I have in mind, a secondary school or schools serving it and the surrounding villages should be placed on one site or campus of thirty to fifty acres, with a county college, medical services and all the facilities for further education and recreation, with playing fields for everybody, including running track, tennis courts, bowling greens. The same kind of 'set-up' could be provided at the centre of a group of villages. Here is a magnificent chance for the counties of England. I estimate that if a well-equipped secondary school can be provided for one pound, you can for twenty-five shillings or, better still, twenty-seven shillings and sixpence provide a satisfactory community centre.

You will see that I have not referred to the host of technical details which in due course will be embodied in building regulations and other documents. What I had wished to do is to make clear the connection between *buildings* for further education and the *concept* of further education. Ideas do govern material. I have claimed, I hope with your agreement, that further education includes the technical, the aesthetic, the corporate and the religious. If buildings in which this concept can be realised are provided everywhere and for all, then we shall be able really to try out what education can do. It will then be realised, I think, that the centre of gravity in the educational system *does* lie in that part of it which provides for youth and maturity.

12
Liberty and the Individual
Introduction

This talk contains certain fairly obvious truths about liberty but Morris has stamped them with his own individual seal. Thus he succeeds in bringing the ideas together in such a way as to promote his firmly held belief that liberty and high standards can best be sustained by organising communities around their cultural institutions and by allowing the participants a major share in the running of these.

He sees a threat to liberty, not from dictators, two of whom had just been eliminated from the European scene, but from the creeping extension of administration and bureaucratic organisation at the expense of the search for quality. He would meet this threat by combining the tradition of the past, stemming from an aristocracy, with a contemporary political idea, an educated democracy, achieving its ends through persuasion and not through coercion.

In this talk he is articulating the ideals which had always informed his thinking and his work. But he was trying to do more than that; he was trying to persuade his listeners that they should accept his thesis, his ideals. He very nearly succeeds.

Liberty and the Individual
Broadcast on the Home Service of the BBC,
13 November 1946

First of all I want to say this: that it is of the greatest importance that we should get quite clear in our minds that, whatever happens in other worlds, it is the plain truth that in the world of values victory is never won once and for all. For instance, take the gift of freedom which like love and many other things are the breath of life to us. This freedom has to be won daily. And perpetual vigilance is the coin with which we have to pay for it. The fact that this is so, lies in the very nature of life and ought not to be the cause of surprise or complaint on our part. We might say that life is a tension and a process involving *re*-formation, struggle and change, not least in the highest forms of excellence, such as the pursuit of goodness, of truth and of beauty. The perfection that involves *no* struggle, which some of us desire, mainly in our moments of weariness and discouragement, cannot be found in life, but only in death. Moreover, here is a point to remember, what we call progress does not mean that life becomes easier. It may mean, for instance, that we have solved one problem only to find ourselves confronted with a more difficult one, making far greater demands on our human originality and energy. Thus, we have every hope of solving the problem of poverty, but only to be confronted by the subtler and, as some think, more terrifying problem of plenty and surfeit. It is still going to be difficult for the well-fed and well-clothed to enter the Kingdom of Heaven. Then again, progress may mean that we pass from a simpler to a more complex stage of the same problem. I think we shall find an example of this process when we come to consider liberty in relation to the individual and the community.

Now freedom is a problem of the ages, discussed without end by philosophers; and so at most I can only hope to touch on an aspect or two which seem to me to have a peculiar relevance to the changed scene of present-day England and the world. We shall save time by admitting that social freedom cannot be had without some organisation, though on the other hand, too much organisation may kill freedom. Even a large degree of automatic action may be the necessary basis of the highest life. We mustn't forget that as human beings a basis of unconscious reflex action, such as breathing and digestion, and of acquired automatic actions, like bicycling, are a condition of bodily and mental freedom. Our very personal careers cannot be ordered and integrated without a plan or an objective. 'Me this unchartered freedom tires', cries Wordsworth in the *Ode to Duty*, 'I feel the weight of chance desires.' So the lives of men and women must be governed by those permanent values and imperatives whose service, strangely enough, is perfect freedom. Clearly, if you take the social sphere alone, organisation is indispensable in the world. It has always been so. How, then, does the present differ from the past? I suggest that it does differ in a profoundly significant way. Our present civilisation is a technological civilisation which has made possible an indefinite multiplication of *means* and has vastly extended the range of consumption and indulgence, and activity for activity's sake.

Now in my view, the characteristic of our time, the mark of a technological civilisation, is the disproportionate growth of administration, is the disproportionate growth of administration and organisation in relation to quality, and, I must say it, the growth of administration as an end in itself. I see this trend as one of the great dangers of our age, and this vast increase of administration has not meant that we are culturally better off. I think we would agree that there was more genius and originality in Tudor and Stuart England than there is in the modern United States with 20 times the population. Not only in commerce, but in local and national social services, we find a growth of administration as an end in itself. I'm afraid this baneful development is very evident in public education. More and more the control of our education tends to be administrative rather than cultural. That this should be so in a matter which is so essentially one of quality, as education undoubtedly is, shows how easily we may become hag-ridden by administration. The view that I want to put to you is that in every part of the social system administration is only safe when it is in the hands of the philosopher and thinker, the teacher, the artist and the saint, for whom administration exists merely as the instrument for realising quality and value. Such people are always economical in their use of administration; for them three-parts of quality goes with one-part of administration. On the contrary, in our contemporary world it often happens that we have three-parts of administration to one-part of quality. We're always lauding that modern invention the practical man, but I look on him as a man who practices administration without regard to quality and ends, and as such in some way a threat to our society. One of the greatest administrators of our time was the philosopher Lord Haldane. Amongst other things he recreated our army. After all if we get down to fundamentals it is the men and women of imagination who are the most practical; it is they who discover fire, electricity, penicillin.

Our age in this country, whether we like it or not, is the age of democracy and the danger that besets democracy is the lack of standards and quality, the lack of spiritual freedom, an addiction to the commonplace, and a tolerance of organisation pursued for its own sake. In referring to our lack of spiritual freedom I'm not forgetting the other important freedoms, economic, political and social.

In the conditions of modern democracy in this country, where can we turn to secure, not one, but all these kinds of freedom? I suggest that it is in the environment of local communities which have become educational societies. Let me explain. During the past few generations there has been a progressive breakdown of sanctions, intellectual and moral, and a collapse of cultural standards. The growth of passive, commercialised amusement and of mere superstition is to me terrifying. Three out of four of us live in towns; in most of our towns ugliness is accepted as normal, beauty regarded as a luxury or even eccentric. There is only one course open to us. Our local communities, whether in the country or in the towns, must be built around their cultural institutions. These cultural institutions must provide for the whole family. In adult education we must include, not only attendance at lectures and laboratories, technology and examinations, but the theatre, the orchestra, the choir and the dance; the consumption and practice of all the Arts in buildings which are themselves works of architectural art; recreation of the body; and finally, the corporate life in common-room, library and hostel. I myself would include places for worship, silence and meditation, where we can nourish the sense of the sacred and the eternal. As the philosopher Whitehead has said: 'The life of man is founded on technology, science, art and religion. All four are inter-connected and issue from his total mentality.' I suggest that it is in such communities, living as educational societies, that we shall have the best chance of relating, in their proper proportions, organisation to freedom, and administration to quality. Indeed there is no other way left.

So I put it to you that the final objective of our town and country planning must be cultural if we are to show democracy is as capable of creating and sustaining cultural values as were the aristocracies of the past. If we do not achieve this in the new towns that Mr Silkin proposes, then England will miss her opportunity and the world and civilisation will be the poorer for it. England looks both ways; on the one hand, to a rich past of political experience, of local government and of freedom of societies within the State; on the other hand, to the future as a socialised democracy. I believe that England is uniquely situated to demonstrate to the world a liberal democracy based on education and its cultural institutions. Moreover, so long as our intellectual method remains one of persuasion and consent it will be an England capable of creating and maintaining freedom, whether political or spiritual, intellectual or aesthetic. I must remind you – since it's relevant – of a final conviction which Plato came to towards the end of his life. He held that the divine element in the world is to be conceived as a persuasive agency and not as a coercive agency. This doctrine, says Professor Whitehead, should be looked upon as one of the greatest intellectual discoveries in the history of religion.

Heaven knows, England has many tasks which she has to do; but this task, going down to the very roots of life itself, she must do in the interests of herself and the world. It is not impossible. To paraphrase Shelley's words in his great essay on Poetry: 'What we have to do is to invest our knowledge with imagination and then have the courage to translate our imagination into fact'. Then again as Bacon has it:

'When a thing is to be done, men ask why it should be done; when it has been done, they ask why it was not sooner done'.

Now before I close, let me go over a few of the points I've made. In my opinion, the grand task of education is frankly to convert society into an infinite number of local cultural communities. The most far-reaching development of education in this country will come from regarding it, not only as a matter of children and schools, but also as the core of social and political philosophy. Thus, education will become the fundamental *principle* and cultural institutions the essential *material* of concrete social organisation. Our communities, whether in town or country must be assembled round their cultural institutions. I would put it this way; that the disorder, the lack of unity and architecture in the *invisible* order of values is reflected in the disorder, the lack of unity and architecture in the *visible* order of our environment. If education were thus corporately administered it could be the principle of unity by which modern communities could be significantly integrated at any stage of culture in east or west. Such, I believe, is the ultimate form of social organisation, and the one best able to create and preserve freedom of whatever kind.

13

Education, Community Centres and other cultural institutions

Introduction

Location and grouping of sites

In 1947 Henry Morris started working two days a week as adviser on new towns in the Ministry of Town and Country Planning. This is a paper prepared for meetings with the various Development Corporations of the new towns, nine of which were being planned and built, under the aegis of the ministry. It is dated from the Ministry of Town and Country Planning 5 March 1948.

'It cannot be said that Henry's advocacy of what was needed in the new towns fell on very fertile ground.' Norman Fisher (1965). This was an understatement. The blank space in the title would be filled in with the name of any new town whose Development Corporation was prepared to listen to him (many were not). But the paper, even though at the time largely disregarded, has a message for planners today.

Some of his critics at the time suggested that Morris may have provided rural Cambridgeshire with village colleges, but he did not appreciate the demands of an urban environment. In spite of his deep attachment to the countryside he had always recognised however that civilised values and civic virtues stemmed from the 'civis', the city itself. True he detested and criticised the contemporary industrial cities, 'squalid and chaotic dormitories sicklied o'er with commercialised amusement', but he was confident that this could be changed, especially in the new towns, by wise planning and inspired architecture. This was why, at first, he looked forward so eagerly to his work as adviser to the minister.

Little remains as written evidence of the work he did, other than notes of meetings he held with the managers of the new towns, and with the education officers of the localities where these were being built. Sometimes these notes give away more than intended as to the negative or even hostile reaction which he met, and which, to be truthful, he sometimes engendered through his manner.

The paper which follows shows his vision and also his style. His approach was, as ever, meticulous but his prescriptions have about them an inflexibility resulting from his conviction that he was right; this must explain in part his lack of success. However the vision remains, along with a typical expression of sensitivity. This is shown in the concern he expresses for the young mother transported from her familiar city street to a new neighbourhood in the new town, lonely and housebound. He noted that 'she practically disappeared from the social scene'. All too little was done at the time for such people, often single parents. But it is worth noting that today, in many different areas of Britain where community education is well developed, crèches are provided and activities organised for these too often forgotten members of the community.

And as for the vision, who but he could have put forward the suggestion that St Mark's Square in Venice might well be a model for the city centre of the new town of Stevenage, Hemel Hempstead or Peterlee. For here, as in St Mark's, a collection of fine buildings would bring together education and administration, the arts and the law in a harmonious architectural and cultural symmetry. Translated into contemporary terms he was only pleading for the association of education with ordinary life, and for both to be closely concerned with the arts and with civic government.

Education, Community Centres and other cultural institutions

Paper prepared for the...Development Corporation, 5 March 1948

I This preliminary memorandum deals with the size, location and, wherever necessary, the grouping of sites for education (primary, secondary, further, community centres) and other cultural institutions, such as the town library, the art gallery, the theatre and the concert hall. It is intended amongst other things to assist the corporation in settling these matters with the local education authority in so far as they are concerned. It is remembered that the L.E.A. is the statutory provider of educational services, subject to the approval of the Minister of Education, each being concerned financially with capital and maintenance expenditure on approximately a fifty–fifty basis. At the same time, it is essential that the corporation, in negotiating with the local education authority on the one hand and on the other in its relation to the Ministry of Education, either by way of informal approach or by formal appeal, should have a thought out policy, and that it should not be merely dependent on the local education authority and the Ministry of Education.

II The location and, wherever necessary, the grouping of educational buildings and buildings for allied cultural or social services is of major importance if one of the major objectives of the new town is to be cultural. Such groupings provide one of the few available opportunities of giving the modern town a significant form and atmosphere. The chance for architectural composition, not only at the centre but at other points in the town, is obvious. Other important advantages that accrue from grouping will be noted in subsequent paragraphs of the memorandum.

III The types of education provided for are as follows:
    nursery schools (2–5 years)
    infant schools (5–7 years)
    junior schools (7–11 years)
    Secondary schools:
        modern schools (11–16 years)
        technical schools (11–18 years)
        grammar schools (11–18 years)
    county colleges (15–18 years)
    further education (includes community centres)
    special schools for handicapped children (5–16 years).

IV A table follows (Schedule A) giving details of school provision from 2 to 18 years for a town of 60,000. The estimates are based on an allowance of 16 school children in each year for each 1,000 of the population. This figure has been arrived at after a recent consultation with officers of the Ministry of Education.

    The acreage required for the services listed in Schedule A is given in Schedule B.

V *Nursery schools (2–5 years)*
The total number of children to be accommodated in each nursery unit is 40. These units should be scattered throughout the town, and in any case not more than *three* units of 40 children each should be placed on the same site. Not less than half an acre is required for each nursery unit. The number of children in a town of 60,000 who may be expected to attend a nursery school is 50 per cent of the age group (i.e. 2,880 ÷ 2 = 1,440). It should be borne in mind, however, that such a service, especially if the units are well distributed and easily accessible to homes, will become very popular and that the number of children of 2–5 years who will *ultimately* attend will be more than 50 per cent of the age group.

    Careful attention should be given to the possibility of grouping maternity and child welfare services with the nursery school units. If this is done some extension of the site would have to be considered.

    The young parent. Thought should be given to one great need of the young parent, particularly the young mother, which is now practically never met. It is found by those who are connected with education and other social services that the young mother, especially the working-class mother, bringing up a young family practically disappears from the social scene. She is tied to the home and generally can only leave it if she takes her young child or children with her. The young parents can seldom go out and do things together. This predicament is becoming common to parents at many social levels. If the young mother and the young married couple are to get their proper cultural and social opportunities in the new towns, then provision must be made for a service of 'watchers' and of day and evening nurseries. Such nurseries might best be grouped with the nursery school and the infant welfare centre.

Infant schools (5–7 years)
For the purposes of location and size of site the number of children that may go to private schools may be ignored and need only be considered when the plans for actual building are under preparation. The Ministry of Education's pamphlet, *The Nation's Schools*, says of infant schools: 'A total of 200 is quite large enough for normal work and 300 should seldom if ever be exceeded'. For an infant school of not less than 200, the size of the site for buildings only is two acres, with extra ground, at the discretion of the local education authority, for small gardens and other activities requiring a grass surface.

It is recommended that an appropriate number of nursery units (say three) should be related to a more or less centrally situated infant school to which they will be contributory.

Junior schools (7–11 years)
If the schools are to be very easily accessible to the homes and not too large, then the solution is to have approximately twelve schools.

Careful consideration should be given to the grouping of each infant school with a junior school on the same site. The individuality of each school would be preserved. Apart from administrative advantages (e.g. servicing) they would provide an architectural grouping which would have some significance for the surrounding neighbourhood.

VI Secondary and further education and allied cultural and social services

(1) Grouping at the town's centre
A college of further education for students of all ages from 18 years and upwards will be provided for the town as a whole. Such a college

Schedule A

Town of 60,000

1,000 population produces 16 children in each school year. Number of children in each school year in a town of 60,000 population: 60 × 16 = 960

Type of school	Age range	Percentage attending	Yearly intake	Total no. of pupils	Size of schools	Form entry	Number of schools
Nursery	2–5 (3 years' course)	50%	480	1,440	40	–	36
Infants	5–7 (2 years' course with margin for 4+)	100%	960	2,160	180–200	2 form + (40 per form)	12
Juniors	7–11 (4 years' course)	100%	960	3,840	320	2 form (40 per form)	12
Secondary Modern	11–16 (5 years' course)	70%	672	3,360	600	4 form (30 per form)	6
Technical	11–18 (7 years' course)	10%	96	672	630	3 form (30 per form)	1
Grammar	11–18 (7 years' course)	20%	192	1,344	630	3 form (30 per form)	2
County Colleges	15–18 (3 years' course) or	70%	672	2,016	135 per day	–	3
	16–18 (2 years' course)	70%	672	1,344	90 per day	–	3

Note: It should be noted that the actual number and sizes of the infant and junior schools will have to be settled in relation to the population of the area served; the total number of school places will not be affected.

Schedule B

Town of 60,000

Type of school	Size of school	Acreage for buildings and playground	Acreage for playing fields	Acreage for other purposes	Total acreage per school	Number of schools	Total acreage
Nursery (2–5)	40	$\frac{1}{2}$	–	–	$\frac{1}{2}$	36	18
Infants (5–7)	180 (2 form entry +)	2	–	–	2	12	24
Juniors (7–11)	320 (2 form entry)	2	$3\frac{3}{4}$	1 (garden)	$6\frac{1}{4}$	12	75
Secondary							
Modern (11–16)	600 (4 form entry)	$3\frac{1}{2}$	13	4 (garden) (boys' school only)	$25\frac{1}{2}$	3 (boys) 3 (girls)	141
Technical (11–18)	630 (3 form entry)	$3\frac{3}{4}$	18	–	$21\frac{3}{4}$	1	$21\frac{3}{4}$
Grammar (11–18)	630 (3 from entry)	$3\frac{3}{4}$	18	–	$21\frac{3}{4}$	2	$43\frac{1}{2}$
County College	135 per day	2	–	–	2	3	6
Community Centre	–	2	8	–	10	3	30

will doubtless also feed some of the rural region around the town, since technical and art education tends to be a *regional* service. The scope of the college will include science and technical education and the humanities (art, literature and drama, music). It will make provision for the corporate life through common-rooms and dining rooms, and for physical recreation through playing courts, playing fields and swimming pool. The courses for Science and the Arts will be both full-time and part-time and will be of a systematic character.

The college of further education ought to be an important and significant part of the central square or squares, where the administrative and the cultural should, so to speak, be blended. Thus there should be a close association between the college of further education, and the art gallery, the concert hall and the town's main library, all three of which will be conceived on livelier and more imaginative lines than in the past. These buildings should have some relation to the town's administrative centre, so that in the result education will not be separated from the active appreciation and practice of the Arts and all of them will not be entirely divorced from civic administration. One example of what might be aimed at is to be found in St Mark's Square at Venice with the Doge's palace, the cathedral, the courts of justice, the library, municipal offices, etc., surrounding perhaps the most potent and moving space in Europe. The theatre has also to be remembered. There is no need to be dogmatic about the actual form of the location of these public buildings in addition to the law court and other administrative buildings. It is possible for them to be placed in very significant relationship even if they are placed in two communicating squares or spaces. The important thing that has been said is to associate education with ordinary life and both with the practice of the Arts and with civic administration.

The question of the size of the site for the building arises. There is no regulation laid down by the ministry and the area will depend on whether the college will have a regional function or not. It is provisionally recommended that approximately four acres should be reserved for the college building. This would allow for some accommodation for fives, racquets, etc. The playing fields would not be at the town centre, but placed at some reasonably accessible spot and should be not less than 14 acres.

(2) *Grouping of secondary education, county college, community centre, etc.*
It is strongly recommended that consideration should be given to the grouping of secondary schools, the county college, further education, including the community centre, the branch library and perhaps the

health centre. Three campuses are suggested, each placed at a selected point between the centre and the periphery of the town and each serving approximately a third of the population. Such centres would be very accessible to the users and would lend very great significance, both cultural and architectural, to the body of the town. For the purposes of ready reference, the three campuses may be lettered A, B and C.

For a town of 60,000 there might be three *selective* secondary schools (one three-form entry grammar school for some 630 boys, one three-form entry grammar school for some 630 girls, and one three-form entry technical high school for some 630 boys *and* girls. These schools would not be placed in isolation in various points near the centre of the town. The boys' grammar school would be on A campus, the girls' grammar school would be on B campus and the technical high school would be on C campus.

At *each* campus, A, B and C, there would be placed two modern schools, one for boys and one for girls, each to serve approximately a third of the town area.[1]

The location and the curriculum of the county college are problems about which no clear lead has been given by the Ministry of Education and in the country generally there is difference of opinion. The truth is that there is more than one answer to both problems and that there is room for experiment. The number of boys and girls of 15–18 in a town of 60,000 who will attend the county college on one day a week will be about 2,000 (400 pupils a day).

Apart from day work, the county college is intended to provide club life for young people in the evenings and at weekends. Clearly, there are serious objections to providing for the whole group of 2,000 in one centre, either in isolation (since the county college ought to be in a context that looks towards maturity) or on the same site as the college of further education. An evening concourse of 500 to 1,000 young people would be a mob rather than a club; and the clubs should be an intimate and human unit in which the young man or young woman can feel that they are really known and matter. It is therefore suggested that the county college should be divided into three units, one to be

1 This memorandum has in mind the allocation of sites from a long-term point of view. Therefore the suggestions for the modern school assume a school leaving age of 16 (not 15) and a school leaving age of 18 for everybody attending the selective grammar and technical high schools. The three year age range (15–18) for the county college is assumed because it is anticipated that the county colleges will be established before very long. Development plans for further education are now being prepared by all local education authorities. When the school leaving age is raised to 16 the age range will be reduced by one year, but it is not thought that the county college building accommodation will then prove excessive.

placed on each of the three campuses where its association with the community centre would provide a context looking towards maturity. Each unit would provide for between six and seven hundred young people. Here would be provided a training on one day a week for each boy and girl in continued education and practical activities, as set out in paragraph 105 'The aims of the County College' of the Ministry of Educations's pamphlet *Youth's Opportunity: Further Education in County Colleges*. There would be some vocational training both in the day time and in the evening, but specific vocational education of a systematic and advanced character would be provided at the college of further education to which selected boys and girls from trades and callings (e.g. printing, building, dress-design) could be sent. While accommodation, including club rooms, would be specially set apart for the county college group at each campus, there would be certain facilities which could be shared in common, e.g. gymnasia, playing fields, tennis, fives and squash courts, etc.).

(3) *The community centre*

This would have some buildings of its own (e.g. branch library, adult lecture rooms, common-rooms, games rooms and a committee room are essential), but as it would be placed near the secondary school many of the rooms belonging to the latter, e.g. workshops, domestic science rooms, laboratories, etc., would be available for use by adults in the evenings. The community centre would provide for young people and adults of all ages a balanced programme of classes and courses at a less systematic level than at the town's college of further education. There would be provision for crafts and hobbies, for instrumental music and singing, and for drama.

The drama will not take its proper place in education, both in the secondary schools and in further education, unless a theatre is available. The customary school hall with a stage at the end has long been obsolete. It should be replaced by a theatre or auditorium with sloping floor and a properly equipped stage. Such an auditorium could be used for drama, music, the film, assemblies, prize days, meetings. It would be used by the secondary schools, the county college and the grown-ups and would make the drama, the opera and orchestral music a reality in public education. The dining rooms will provide for those activities that require a flat floor.

Consideration should be given to the possibility of placing a Health Centre under the Ministry of Health on each campus site and of associating the School Medical Service in the same building with the Health Centre.

(4) *The advantages of grouping*

Reference has already been made to the advantage from the point of view of significance and architectural design of grouping the further education facilities on three campus sites. Another important consideration should be emphasised. The multilateral school is still a very controversial issue. The course recommended in this memorandum is to give the modern schools and the grammar schools and the technical high school the same standard of buildings and amenities and to put them in association on the same campus. Thus the grammar school will not be isolated, and the three types of secondary school will be placed in an identical physical context. They would have many contacts as, for example, in meeting each other on the football field, in debate and perhaps in choruses, opera, drama and orchestra. The three schools might have the same coat of arms with a slight deviation for the modern school, the grammar school and the technical high school. It is suggested that serious consideration should be given to the provision of a fine chapel at each campus, to be used jointly by all the secondary schools. As is well known, morning assembly and religious teaching are now compulsory in all publicly maintained schools.

There are certain administrative advantages in the grouping of secondary education on the campus. There are possible capital economies at the beginning in such things as drainage, and economies in maintenance administration such as caretaking and heating, and the servicing of playing fields and grounds.

Size of campus sites

The total acreage required for the educational services set out in Schedule B amounts to 81 acres [*sic*]. This is a provisional estimate.

If a health centre were added there will have to be a comparatively small addition. There is no need to make any specific provision for the branch library building. It should be noted that provision is made for an 8-acre recreation ground for the adults attending the community centre. This should be borne in mind in considering what provision should be made in the plan for the public recreation grounds.

Sites for special schools

Provision in the plan should be made for the following schools for handicapped children:

(1) A special school for delicate and physically handicapped children (5 acres);

(2) A special school for educationally sub-normal children (5 acres).

14

Architecture, Humanism and the Local Community

Introduction

Morris was asked to give a talk at the R.I.B.A. in May 1956. Later that year he was invited to become an Associate of the Institute. 'There is nothing,' he wrote to a friend at the time, 'I could have liked better.'

'It fascinates me that he spoke at the R.I.B.A. in 1956 on community schools and no one really heard what he was saying, and now, suddenly, it all starts up as if he were alive.' Henry Swain, Chief Architect of Nottinghamshire (1972).[1]

Here is that R.I.B.A. talk. As so often, Morris has lifted occasional paragraphs from talks he had made previously to very different audiences. However they fit comfortably into the structure of this one which includes also some important original proposals and ideas.

Although he remains aware that he is speaking to a professional audience whose skills he does not share, he underlines the fact that architecture is the most public of all the arts and therefore is saddled with weighty responsibility. For him, this responsibility to the wider world focuses on education as he himself saw it and preached it. It is here that his ideal – education seen as a life-long experience extending far beyond the classroom, far beyond academic learning – becomes linked with the material expression of that ideal in buildings; buildings which should be planned and conceived with that ideal in mind. His conception of the planner as being much more than an expert in positioning drains, roads and buildings is matched here with his idea of an architect as someone more than a designer, who is an artist as well as an engineer, co-operating with painters, sculptors, and other craftsmen. At the same time he stresses the need for architects to be aware of the social and cultural pressures which are exerted by their completed work. These are the lessons which he, ever the teacher, was putting across in this talk. Clearly, at least with one county architect, he succeeded.

[1] Swain was responsible for the building of Sutton Centre, at Sutton in Ashfield, one of the most notable architectural and educational successes of our time.

Architecture, Humanism and the Local Community

Paper read to the Royal Institute of British
Architects, 15 May 1956, published in R.I.B.A.
Journal, June 1956

The age of industrialism and democracy has brought to an end most of the great cultural traditions of Europe, and not least that of architecture. In the contemporary world in which the majority are half-educated and not many even a quarter-educated, and in which large fortunes and enormous power can be obtained by exploiting ignorance and appetite, there is a vast cultural breakdown which, as we approach universal literacy, will stretch from America to Europe and from Europe to the East. One effect of the breakdown to which I refer is to be seen in the disintegration of the visual environment in highly civilised countries in Europe with a long tradition of humanised landscape occupied by villages and towns of architectural character, sometimes of moving beauty. The march of squalor proceeds from the Eastern hemisphere to Africa and then to the West. In its grimmest and most cruel form it is to be found in industrialised countries, for instance in large parts of the United States.

The kind of visual environment which upholds and dignifies the episode of man is being destroyed in old countries like our own, and it is simply not being created in countries all over the world which are now being, or are about to be, industrialised. I do not stop to diagnose the reasons for this collapse and failure or discuss what the remedies may be. I hasten to point out that we are about to be confronted with another disabling deprivation in our surroundings. Let me first point out the extent to which the quantitative, the impersonal, the non-human is becoming almost wholly the condition of existence in a society whose main instrument is applied science and technology. This impersonal mechanical element is invading and dominating all spheres, the economic, the political and the social. I need only to mention nuclear science, automation, electronics, the monolithic state, giant industrial combines, speed, noise, the enormous proliferation of administration. (Up to 1916 the British Cabinet, which was engaged in governing not only these islands but the Empire, met regularly without an agenda and kept no minutes of its proceedings.) We are only at the beginning of this revolution in the life of man. Before long the whole of humanity on this planet will have passed from an agricultural and hand-craft civilisation to a highly industrialised technological civilisation.

I ought at this point to explain that I mean by architecture the ordering of the whole of our visual environment, and in architecture thus conceived I include not only the architect, the engineer and the craftsman, but also the sculptor, the painter and the landscapist. One of the main functions of architecture in high civilisation has been to give significance to man's physical environment, either in terms of feeling through awe and the numinous (the sense of what is hallowed and sacred) or in terms of the human body and its manifold physical states – all of these being humane values of great importance and efficacy in the psychological, emotional and physical life of man. As Geoffrey Scott has said, we transcribe ourselves into terms of architecture: also, we transcribe architecture into terms of ourselves. The whole of architecture is in fact unconsciously invested by us with human movement and human moods. This is the humanism of architecture.

I am referring to all that in Well Building forms part of the quality and condition of *delight*.

What all this has meant in the life of man by giving it meaning and the wonder of an ubiquitous humane incarnation is not to be expressed, except perhaps in an utterance which itself would be a work of art. I trench here on the supreme importance of architecture in the life of man because of its public character. It is our subtlest form of compulsory aesthetic education.

I stand before you this evening as one convinced intellectually, technically and aesthetically not only of the inevitability of new forms of modern architecture, but eager and enthusiastic to embrace this chance of a new beginning. In this case the inevitable must not merely be accepted; it must be embraced. Such realism has always been a condition of an original flowering of art forms. The conjugation of the forms of architecture that have been traditional for some three thousand years has become feeble and dies in the presence of the new possibilities of structure and material now available to us. The functional and stylistic revolution of architecture has begun and will become universal. I will refer later to the changes in the social scene which have relevance for architecture. What I would like now to say as a layman is that modern architecture has made great advances in structural originality and in interior functional efficiency and aesthetic efficacy. It has not yet fully developed that external function of delight which the architecture of Europe has performed and which has to be replaced. I am thinking not only of the serving of humane values which Greek and Roman Renaissance architecture and the classically informed architecture of England has performed down to Regency times. I am thinking also of the spatial arrangements that constitute the precinct in its various geometrical forms which have given delight and security to man's daily life.

Not only has modern architecture, I suggest, not yet begun to perform what I should call its external service to the local community, one gets the impression that architects are not sufficiently aware of this service as an imperative and a necessity. I have mentioned those states of psychological and physical pleasure which in the past it has been the external function of architecture to evoke. Modern architects have to search and experiment to find out how far the structural possibilities of modern materials are capable of performing externally this humane, sensuous, and aesthetic function. It is difficult for a layman to see how modern architecture may throw up decorative themes which are but discarded functional devices. Time alone, I suppose, can show that. What is crystal clear is that the expression of humane values in architecture depends more than ever on the architect continuing to be an artist as well as an engineer co-operating with other artists – painters, sculptors, designers of tapestry, and craftsmen. And the creation of these conditions of delight can be quite separate from structural forms and additional to such structural forms as may be found to have aesthetic and humane value.

I would venture to urge that modern architecture should not hesitate to use the geometrical forms that create the local precinct, the square, the three-sided court, the circle, the crescent, and that in doing so it will not involve itself in the futility of imitation. These forms have a continuing social use and convenience as well as aesthetic influence. There may be, awaiting discovery, other forms of capturing and organising space for the pleasure of man.

It is obvious too that the elaboration of external texture both as to form and colour will continue to be a method of giving humane values to architecture. I have spoken of the condition of *delight* in Well Building. I hasten to note, with emphasis, that it is still within the power of architects to invest modern structures, both within and without, with the sense of awe and the numinous which is the essential character of religious architecture. I believe that Mr Basil Spence will create a cathedral at Coventry which internally and externally will be invested with these qualities of the awesome and of the numinous as intense and moving as those to be found in the greatest of existing churches.

Again, in this world of increasing impersonality and sameness we must hold before our minds and imaginations the humane value in architecture of the unique work of art, the unique work of sculpture, whether fixed or free, the unique mural decoration, the unique fixed painting or tapestry, the aesthetic use of water in the unique fountain.

I sum up in a sentence the main contention I have tried to make. It is a profound necessity for civilisation that modern architecture should discharge its external function of ennobling and giving significance to our environment and to do so in terms of humanist values.

I pass on now to another aspect of the problem of creating and preserving in our environment the individual, the idiosyncratic, the idiomatic, the humane, in a world in which the anonymous and the impersonal increasingly envelop us. I am thinking of something physical, the *locality* (the creation and design of which is the architect's gift to us), and of something social, the *local community*.

Up to almost half-way through the nineteenth century only the governing minorities of societies were literate. Now not only Europe and North America but the whole planet is becoming literate. It is safe to assume that by the end of the twentieth century everyone, except the mentally defective, will be able to read and write. At the same time, science and technology are being applied to all the processes of life. It is in this circumstance that our civilisation, both of the masses and of the minorities, differs from all previous civilisations. Applied science will bring food, clothing, health and convenience to the undeveloped countries, as it has brought those benefits to existing industrialised countries. But technology and industrialism not only revolutionise agriculture – they kill the culture and the magical art which in rural societies sprang up side by side with agriculture. Where the victory of technology is complete, as in North America, the numinous is never created, and the numinous is a major condition of creative art in the experience of our race so far. In old countries like China and India the conditions of the numinous are being destroyed on a rapid and enormous scale; in countries like England, France and Italy the numinous is evaporating. Urban man, whether he lives in garden cities or the industrial slums, loses natural religion, his songs, music and legends, and the ritual dance.

What happens to industrialised man? He kills leisure time with amusement and, be it noted, amusement mainly passive and largely commercialised – professional sport, the cinema, the radio, television, football pools, gambling, newspaper reading, etc. – which excites and distracts but seldom or never recreates or gives instinctive satisfaction or happiness. 'Small wonder that Monsieur Bergson has called ours an 'aphrodisiac civilisation'. But the epithet is not quite just. It is not that we worship Aphrodite. If we did, we should fear these make-believes as a too probable cause of her wrath. An aphrodisiac is taken with a view to action: photographs of bathing girls are taken as a substitute for it. The truth may rather be that these things reveal a society in which sexual passion has so far decayed as to have become no longer a god, as for the Greeks, or a devil, as for the early Christians, but a toy: a society where the instinctive desire to propagate has been weakened by a sense that life, as we have made it, is not worth living, and where our deepest wish is to have no posterity.' (Collingwood: *The Principles of Art*.)

Is it possible in any way to counter this habit of passive amusement which envelops man everywhere, and to give him the opportunity for activity of body and mind, and active mental, sensuous and emotional experience?

Our species, in solving the problem of poverty and overwork, is in fact moving forward to a more difficult and perilous stage in its history. For what is called social progress, we have now learned, is not a movement towards a static perfection; it is the exchanging of one set of solved problems for a new and more significant set of problems making greater demands on human originality and energy. The solution of the economic problem awaits no longer so much on knowledge as on an effort of political will and administration. Universal comfort, with wealth and repletion and with large margins of free time, is the next great problem of *homo sapiens*. The human house will indeed be swept and garnished for a fresh fate. Words cannot do justice to the urgency and the wisdom of thinking our now new institutions to enable communities to face this new situation. To do this we must arm ourselves with two conceptions which are, in fact, complementary. First, adult education is the major part of education. The centre of gravity in the public system of education should reside in that part which provides for youth and maturity. Secondly, the fundamental principle and the *final* object of all future community planning everywhere, whether urban or rural, should be cultural.

Planning is almost universally conceived of in terms mainly of the reorganisation of the economic and instrumental services of community life – industry, transport, housing, sanitation, water, light and amenities. Planning must provide, not only for the economic and instrumental order, but also for the cultural and social life of the community conceived in its widest sense. Apart from the programme of the schools up to the age of eighteen, those cultural objects are religion, the practice of mental and physical health, adult education, science and the humanities, social and physical recreation in community centres, and the consumption and practice of all the arts by adults whether in groups or individually. The most fruitful and far-reaching development of education in our generation will come as a result of conceiving of it not only as a matter of psychology but also as the core of social and political philosophy; and of regarding education as the fundamental principle, and educational institutions as the essential material of concrete social organisation. The organisation of communities around their educational institutions is capable of universal application in any society and at any stage of culture. It is also the ultimate form of social organisation. It is the only method of escape from the impasse of modern society, in which some unity of communal life is necessary, but in which, by the operation of freedom of thought, a multiplicity of autonomous associations has grown up side by side with the State and replaced a single dominant view of life. A pluralistic society has taken the place of a monistic society, and architecture, both in the invisible hierarchy of values and in the visual order of our environment, is difficult or impossible to achieve. Some method for the integration of the life of the community with vital relevance to modern conditions is the prime social necessity of our age. The unity of social and spiritual life with its institutional and civic expression in architecture and organisation which was characteristic of the mediaeval town and the parish church and manor of the countryside has gone for ever. But the effect, in modern times, of pluralism of associations and beliefs has been one of social disintegration, less evident in the village than in the contemporary town with its social fissiparousness and resultant architectural chaos. Since the breakdown of the mediaeval civilisation we have, so far as the social expression of values in communal living is concerned, been living on credit, consisting of the legacies of the forms of the Middle Ages and of the brief and brilliant, but morally impossible, eighteenth century. Today we have to find a principle of integration which will allow unity of communal life and architectural expression and at the same time give free development on which growth and freedom depend. In mediaeval Europe a common organisation for communal living was made possible by a system of common values and beliefs. In our time that element of unity in the life of society which is essential will be attained by the organisation of communities around their educational and cultural institutions. It is by some such synthesis that modern communities can again become organic, that the decay of civic life and architecture could be arrested, and the planning of modern towns on lines of imaginative significance surpassing the achievements of the past, be made possible.

The development, therefore, everywhere and for everybody, of a fully articulated system of adult education is the most important of all the tasks that lie before us. Such a development of adult education would include activities at a number of levels, intellectual, aesthetic, and recreative, with extensive provision for corporate life.

This prompts me to dwell with eagerness on certain implications which I believe have a profound bearing on the community pattern in this or any country. The locality or neighbourhood in which we spend our daily lives and the local community to which we belong form the cell of society. It is of supreme importance that the neighbourhood should be full of life and vitality and have significance and meaning for all those who live in it. But vastly increased transport and opportunities for amusement have weakened the local group and its personal and corporate activities. This has happened as much in the cities as elsewhere. How is this vitality to be realised – this activity of body and mind, of emotion and feeling, both personally and in groups, that is the precious essence and core of culture at any level? It comes about when teacher and student, student and student, young and old meet face to face in lecture and debate, in song and dance; or in orchestras, choirs and plays. I have seen groups absorbed in workshops, laboratories, studios, libraries. And there are the virtues of eating and drinking together and conversation in the common-room, and all that happens in games and on the playing fields and running track. A community that has these things enjoys the deepest satisfactions, which nothing can replace. It has an antidote to one of the greatest dangers of modern life, the pursuit of all kinds of passive mass amusements which kill time rather than recreate.

Adult education and recreation of the kind I have described are as necessary to everybody as food and air. So are the *active* practice and enjoyment of all the arts. I reiterate the belief I formed 34 years ago which has become stronger than ever; it is that the centre of gravity in education and the culture it transmits should be in that part that provides for youth and maturity. How is this to be brought about in the countryside and the cities? One main means to this end is to group our local communities round their colleges and secondary schools. It is plain common sense and wisdom to do this in the new housing estates, the new towns, and the expanded towns which are now being talked about. And it should be done not merely to avoid frustration, loneliness, and boredom, but with the positive intention of creating civilised communities able to live the good life. These colleges and secondary schools are an entirely new thing in our history. They cost vast sums. For instance, in a new town of 60,000 the secondary schools alone cost £1,500,000. In no other country in the world are such magnificent schools now being built. Let us, as the Minister of Education suggests, attach community wings to such colleges and schools so that, with their wealth of facilities, their accommodation and equipment, they can become part of the community pattern and centres of community life.

Such a pattern is valid for the countryside and city in any country at whatever level of culture. All over the world, and especially in Africa and the East, science and technology are being used to abolish poverty, to bring about better food supplies and housing, health and a longer life, and thus to leave behind the life that is nasty, brutish, and short. This is one of the biggest changes taking place in the world today. Nothing can stop it. As Robert Bridges has said, 'They have seen the electric light i' the West' (electricity symbolising the new world of technical invention) as we in the West once saw the star of Christianity in the East. But the application of science to material welfare should take place with a constant regard for human values. I believe that one of the surest ways of doing this, and one ready to hand, is to group communities physically round their cultural institutions so that these can form part of daily life and habit. We must all earn our living and proper training for that is a necessity; but it is also a desperate necessity, and not a luxury, that the satisfaction of the cultural and recreative needs of the local community should be a major aim in town and country everywhere.

I have dealt with the need of men and women in the local community everywhere for institutions to which they can repair to carry on that active personal culture and creative life of body, mind and feeling, which is life at its best and most real.

I return to the physical aspect of the locality. The creation of the locality with its precinctual character is a major task of architecture, but it has been completely forgotten in the speculative building and in the housing estates of the past half-century. Even today the precinctual locality is not provided for in the expansion of existing towns by local authorities. In the conglomeration of long meaningless streets with no social, religious or cultural significance, architecture becomes non-existent. The bus conductor at the terminus of a

Birmingham housing estate cries out *Sahara*, and it is indeed in such social deserts that one feels the full impact of the exclamation of the poet, 'Ah, what a dusty answer gets the soul...' I can make my views more explicit by referring to what has been happening in the new towns.

We can no longer achieve in them the grandeur and impressiveness of domestic architecture such as characterises for instance Bath, Regent's Park and Bloomsbury. If we are to give our new towns and the housing estates architectural significance and a civic sense we are bound to use our educational and cultural buildings as focal points. This involves the imaginative location of colleges, schools, libraries, community centres, art galleries. I am glad to say that in most of the new towns the college of adult education has been placed in the town centre so that it is given a cultural as well as an administrative and commercial character. There may be a theatre and a cinema, a hotel, cafés, restaurants and the open market. Thus the town's central square by day and night may be alive like St. Mark's Square in Venice. This blend of daily life and civic administration with the main cultural buildings is irresistible as a conception and in practice, and continues an ancient tradition of European civilisation.

Likewise the neighbourhood centres, each serving a portion of the town, are spacious precincts for shopping, with an inn, a community centre or hall, the branch library with the large secondary school adjacent or near at hand. Thus, in the new towns, cultural buildings, which are the largest public buildings, have been deliberately located to create an atmosphere of civic significance. In one new town, its nine large secondary schools have been located in groups of three, on three large sites or campuses, lying between the centre and the circumference of the town. Each campus and its buildings, gardens and playing fields is a cultural focal point, lending dignity to the surrounding streets and housing. Even infant and junior schools can be and have been sited so that they are grouped significantly with the surrounding houses.

The majority of our new educational buildings are being built in modern and not traditional terms. It is impossible to overstate the need that such educational buildings should, through their external form, composition and texture, contribute significance to their surroundings. To the extent to which a school building does not serve these humane values it is therefore an architectural and aesthetic failure in an external world that is becoming increasingly impersonal and mechanised. I should like to observe that we may fail to create this humane function in modern architecture if we are too much influenced or dominated by considerations of speed. It is the techniques of rapid building that have done as much as anything to lead architects to sacrifice the humane external function of school buildings. In a decade or two the bad effects of an unnecessary and doctrinaire worship of speed in school buildings will become painfully obvious.

It is with such a policy, it seems to me, that town and country planning and architecture can enable a town or a group of villages to provide not only an environment, but a way of life, in which the personal, the intimate, the humane are given full expression, and where architecture as an art can make its fullest impact on young and old daily and throughout life.

Here let me state a belief which arises out of a working life spent in public education, from the beginning of which I was seized with the vital importance of architecture. That belief is that architecture, as the great public art present to us all during the whole of our waking lives, is part of the essence of education. Architecture, the understanding and particularly the appreciation of it, should occupy as important a part in education at school and in adult life as our English mother tongue and literature.

Let me try to sum up in a sentence or two the views that I have expounded.

We are living in a world dominated by applied science and technology. The necessity for the artist, who sustains humane and personal values, is greater than ever. Certain creations of the artist, such as music, literature and painting, we are able to obtain and enjoy in our private capacities. But architecture as the great public art to whose influence all are subject can only be provided by Society, and be it noted at the hands of the architect who is an artist. Modern architecture, which is the result of new structural principles and materials with a mechanical logic of their own, is confronted with an imperative which it must obey. This is that, in addition to its practical utilitarian functions, modern architecture must nourish humanist values, especially in its external service of expressing the significance of man's activities, of giving nobility to his environment, and ministering to his delight and appetite for beauty. It is not to be contemplated that modern architecture will fail to do this.

The task is indeed formidable. Already we see that the new textures, for the most part, are unresponsive to the unimaginable touch of Time. There are those who fear that the new mechanics of structure and the new materials may defeat the artist. Such is the challenge to modern architecture and such is its creative opportunity.

15
The Idea of a Village College
Introduction

This talk can be seen as his Swan Song. He was over 65, he had been ill with pneumonia, he had retired from Cambridgeshire. 'You've lost your fire, Henry,' said one of his friends rather cruelly at this time. He himself said he had become 'an extinct volcano'. In a letter to a friend written while composing this talk he wrote: 'At present I'm in the throes of writing a broadcast for 9.15 after the news on the Home Programme. The BBC pressed me to do it. It's terribly difficult to get done. I'm so stale about the subject, 'The Idea of the Village College', and I daren't say anything that implies vanity...'

It was in fact a good talk and worthy of that peak listening time. It contains the essence of his philosophy and places the village college neatly in the historical context of his own life-span and of his own career, pursued for more than 30 years in a 'poor corner of rural England'. His description of what was going on in the four colleges already built is perhaps a little rosier than the reality, but only a little and the fault is excusable.

He throws an interesting sidelight on the political climate of his day when the Tory government (with R. A. Butler at Education, to be followed later by David Eccles) was promoting public spending on social and educational activities which they believed were as important as schemes whose sole object was mere economic improvement. While he acknowledges and welcomes the fact that 'science and technology are being used to abolish poverty, to bring about better food supplies and housing, health and a longer life...', he insists characteristically at the end that 'the application of science to material welfare should take place with a constant regard for human values'.

The Idea of a Village College
Talk given on the BBC Home Service, text published in *The Listener*, 10 February 1955

The welfare of agriculture and the countryside is haunted by an anxiety over the drift of people, especially young people, from the country to the cities. This movement has been going on in Britain for more than a century: it happens in all industrialised countries. I think it is generally agreed that (apart from the obvious fact that production of food is a necessity) country life and traditions and country stocks are not merely valuable, they are an indispensable element in any society. Of course, much can be done to enable the countryside to compete with the powerful pull of the city. And it is one aspect of this problem that I wish to discuss – the need for better education and better chances of recreation and social life. The view that I want to put to you is that agriculture must be more than technically and mechanically efficient. It must provide an attractive way of life.

I should like to tell you about my experience in a quiet and rather poor corner of rural England. I well remember the scene in Cambridgeshire 34 years ago. Most villages had a single school for children of all ages up to fourteen. The buildings were mainly old, badly lighted and heated, often insanitary. The windows were high up and nearly always faced the sunless north. The Board of Education issued a 'black list' of school buildings which had either to be ended or mended. And those long, heavy desks in iron frames that only a grown-up could move? The magic of colour had not yet been discovered – grim browns and dark greens were the dominant decoration. Groups of children sat grave and silent with folded arms. Day in and day out, the children listened, the teachers talked; it was education by discourse. In spite of all this the village schoolmasters and schoolmistresses often did remarkable work. Many of them were characters who meant much and did much for village life.

This picture was true of rural England in general, and indeed of the cities, apart, of course, from the grammar schools. Clearly something had to be done about it, not least for the older children – even in those days the raising of the school-leaving age to fifteen was in the air. For youngsters and grown-ups the scene was even bleaker. For all the things they wanted to do, whether serious or gay, the village school building was pretty hopeless. Village halls were few, and mostly poor affairs.

The truth is that the village and the small country town had ceased to be self-sufficient social units. That is one of the main reasons why for so long they have had their faces turned to the cities. 'Each age is a dream that is dying or one that is coming to birth'. It seemed to me, thirty years ago, that the one way of getting rid of this dependence was to provide better education and more recreation and social life at the centres of fairly large rural districts and to use modern transport to make this possible. As we know, one kind of rural district, namely the small market town with its nearby villages, has existed for centuries. Another kind of rural district can be made up of a group of villages centring upon a large village. Given a suitable centre, a better education could be given to the older boys and girls in spacious and well-equipped buildings with playing fields. A much better job, too, would be done for the younger children in their junior schools. And then, at the centre, there would be a chance of making a fine home for all kinds of activities for the older population, a whole range of activities which, until then, were simply out of the question. All this seemed to me to demand what, at the time, was the making of a new institution for the countryside.

And so thirty years ago we planned to group nine villages with a population of 10,000 and to build what became known as a village college in the largest of them, namely Sawston. The first object was to provide a school for the 300 older children of these villages. There was to be a hall for use by the school and as the local theatre and cinema; and many other amenities which by now have become familiar but which 34 years ago seemed something of a dream in the countryside. But we aimed not just at a school but rather at a community centre, equipped throughout so that it could be used not only by a secondary school in the daytime but also grown-ups in the evening. And, mark you, for young people and grown-ups there was also to be a wing consisting of a panelled lecture room with easy chairs; a library and reading room; a common-room with canteen and space for clubs and indoor games of all sorts. So the whole building could be thrown open for use in the evenings and at week-ends to the community of nine villages for a generous programme of adult education, both serious and gay, not forgetting agriculture and horticulture, and for all sorts of recreation.

A Part of Education

I recall the remark of an Oxford scholar, Sir Henry Clay, many years later when visiting a village college on a Saturday afternoon. 'How pleasant,' he exclaimed, as he saw the rabbit show, a wedding reception, a football match and the preparations for an evening dance, 'how pleasant to see so many things going on that have nothing to do with education. Of course,' he added, 'they *are* part of education.'

But where was the money to come from? There were no precedents. The famous Hadow Report about the remaking of the nation's schools had still to come when Sawston was being planned, and the Board of Education would give money only for the barest minimum of what was called elementary education. So to make Sawston possible more than half the cost had to be met by gifts of land, money, and equipment. Without the generosity of the Carnegie Trustees and other benefactors Sawston could not have been built and opened, as it was in 1930, by the Prince of Wales. Three other village colleges, all assisted by substantial gifts of money and in kind, followed at Bottisham, Linton, and Impington. In all four, architecture and landscape, the artist and colour, have been used to create places of beauty within and without. A distinguished historian of architecture, Professor Pevsner of Cambridge University, describes the Impington of Walter Gropius and Maxwell Fry, built in 1939, as 'one of the best buildings of its date in England, if not the best'.

We find that some 70 per cent of the children, after they have left school and gone to work, return in the evenings. People arrive on foot, by cycle, car, and bus. Beside the headmaster, or warden, and his staff there is a governing body for each college, on which everybody who uses the college is represented: the aim is to give as many as possible a chance to take a hand in running the place. The neighbouring villages are not forgotten: classes and other activities are arranged in each of them, too. So there is a two-way service and village life is strengthened. The numbers vary. Impington, the largest, with ten villages and 11,000 people has 1,000 students attending classes weekly and a similar number attending voluntary societies and clubs.

Before the war, much was being done in country and town; but it was the Butler Act of 1944 that gave the complete and explicit sanction to secondary schools for all and to community centres. Bassingbourn Village College is a community centre and secondary modern school for fifteen villages and was built wholly out of public funds under the Butler Act. It was appropriately opened by Mr Butler himself a few months ago. Recently the Minister of Education, Sir David Eccles, has given a clear signal for an advance in school building, especially in the countryside, and has lifted the ban on expenditure for community centres both in town and country.

This prompts me to dwell with eagerness on certain implications which I believe have a profound bearing on the community pattern in this or any country. The locality or neighbourhood in which we spend our daily lives and the local community to which we belong form the cell of society. It is of supreme importance that the neighbourhood should be full of life and vitality and have significance and meaning for all those who live in it. But vastly increased transport and opportunities for amusement have weakened the local group and its personal and corporate activities. This has happened as much in the cities as elsewhere. How is this vitality to be realised – this activity of body and mind, of emotion and feeling, both personally and in groups, that is the precious essence of adult education? It comes about when teacher and student, student and student, young and old meet face to face in lecture and debate, for instance, or in song and dance; again in orchestras, choirs, and plays. I have seen groups absorbed in workshops, laboratories, studios, libraries. And there are the virtues of eating and drinking together and conversation in the common-room, and all that happens in games and on the playing field and running track. A community that has these things enjoys the deepest satisfactions, which nothing can replace. It has an antidote to one of the greatest dangers of modern life, the pursuit of all kinds of passive mass amusements which kill time rather than recreate.

Adult education and recreation of the kind I have described are necessary to everybody as food and air. So are the active practice and enjoyment of all the arts. A belief I formed 34 years ago has become stronger than ever: it is that the centre of gravity in education should be in that part that provides for youth and maturity. How is this to be brought about in the countryside and the cities? One main means to this end is to group our local communities round their colleges and secondary schools. It is plain common sense and wisdom to do this in the new housing estates, the new towns, and the expanded towns which are now being talked about. And it should be done not merely to avoid frustration, loneliness, and boredom, but with the positive intention of creating civilised communities able to live the good life. These colleges and secondary schools are an entirely new thing in our history. They cost vast sums. For instance, in a new town of 60,000 the secondary schools alone cost £1,500,000. In no other country in the world are such magnificent schools now being built. Let us, as the Minister of Education suggests, attach community wings to such colleges and schools so that, with their wealth of facilities, their accommodation and equipment, they can become part of the community pattern and centres of community life.

Such a pattern is valid for the countryside and city in any country at whatever level of culture. All over the world, and especially in Africa and the East, science and technology are being used to abolish poverty, to bring about better food supplies and housing, health and a longer life, and thus to leave behind the life that is nasty, brutish, and short. This is one of the biggest changes taking place in the world today. Nothing can stop it. As Robert Bridges has said, 'They have seen the electric light i' the West' (electricity symbolising the new world of technical invention) as we in the West once saw the star of Christianity in the East. But the application of science to material welfare should take place with a constant regard for human values. I believe that one of the surest ways of doing this, and one ready to hand, is to group communities physically round their cultural institutions so that these can form part of daily life and habit. We must all earn our living, and proper training is a necessity; but it is also a desperate necessity, and not a luxury, that the satisfaction of the cultural and recreative needs of the local community should be a major aim in town and country everywhere.

These, then, are some of the ideas that have developed in my mind from the idea of a village college since Sawston was planned thirty years ago. I end with a saying of Francis Bacon: 'Men...till a matter be done, wonder that it can be done: as soon as it is done, wonder again that it was not sooner done.'

Morris and the Future
His prescriptions and our achievements
by Harry Rée

'We need constantly to remind ourselves of the menace of aimless leisure amidst economic security, and that the decadence and disillusion that will arise with widespread intellectual and emotional unemployment will be more tragic than the sufferings of the long era of restriction and overworked poverty from which we are emerging.' (1936) (See page 53)

'Our species, in solving the problem of poverty and overwork is in fact moving forward to a more difficult and perilous stage in its history... Words cannot do justice to the urgency and the wisdom of thinking out now new institutions to enable communities to face this new situation.' (1943) (See page 80)

The social and economic needs of the future should be a little more obvious to us today than they were to Henry Morris forty or fifty years ago, but we still have a long way to go before it is generally recognised that leisure when aimlessly faced is destructive, or when stigmatised as unemployment is unacceptable. But when that leisure is spent in ways which significate people, through offering them socially meaningful tasks or pastimes, then we have begun to 'face the new situation'. Community education gives us one of the most important ways of doing so.

The institutions which he established in the 'demonstration area' of Cambridgeshire during his lifetime have flourished; in Cambridgeshire today the majority of secondary schools are village or community colleges. Often they have become models of what he envisaged, used seven days a week by young people and adults for learning and leisure with little distinction between the two. At the same time many primary schools there have been encouraged by the local education authority to follow the same course. At the end of the forties the idea jumped over the northern boundary of the county into the then Soke of Peterborough. Here the first village college outside Cambridgeshire was opened at Glinton in 1949; the first Warden came from Linton Village College. Local authority reorganisation has caused the Soke, with Huntingdonshire to become part of Cambridgeshire, and secondary schools in both these former local authorities are now operating as community colleges.

Working in the education offices in Peterborough in 1949 was the young Robert Aitkin. Today, as Director of Education for Coventry, he has been the driving force in establishing the city as one of the leading examples of community education. All the primary and secondary schools are involved, and adolescents and adults in the city regard 'their' schools as places where they can go back to freely, for study or recreation. In fact the city has probably gone further than anywhere else in that each secondary school is under an obligation to keep in touch with students who leave them at 16 for a further two years to offer them advice about jobs or about opportunities for further study or involvement in any other leisure activity.

Coventry is special too because the ever-growing Community Education Development Centre is established there. It is independent and funded jointly by trusts based in the U.S.A. and Holland. The centre initiates numerous projects in various parts of the country where teachers or social workers or other professionals set up schemes for involving people of all sorts and conditions in collective action, perhaps to improve themselves and the quality of their lives, perhaps to improve their families, perhaps to improve their locality. It also advises teachers and administrators as to ways to transform a traditional educational system or a traditional school into one where all members of the community can, if they want to, claim a stake. The centre runs a monthly newspaper, *Network*, which regularly gives information about developments in community education, and news of the ever-expanding Community Education Association. Academic institutions are served from the centre through the *Journal of Community Education* which appears quarterly.

Leicestershire was probably the first big education authority to follow the Cambridgeshire example as county policy, and today, with Coventry, is probably the leader in the field. Again, the influence of the Chief Education Officer was crucial. The late Stewart Mason came to Leicestershire from being an H.M.I. in Cambridgeshire. Here he knew Morris and became a friend and admirer. Extending the village college idea, and publicly acknowledging his debt to Morris, he established colleges in the towns as well as in the countryside, and adopted the title for them of community colleges. His successor, Andrew Fairbairn, has further developed the system. Geographically contiguous, Nottinghamshire soon followed suit. Here the Chief Education Officer, Joe Stone, came directly to his post from Leicestershire, and in co-operation with the county architect Henry Swain, an unashamed admirer of Morris's ideas, set up a system of schools and colleges where district and parish councils were involved in providing facilities inside and next to the buildings planned and put up by the county. Probably the most outstanding and best known of these is at Sutton in Ashfield, where the institution, avoiding the name of school or college is simply known as Sutton Centre; it was opened in 1973. Before plans were sketched out or even discussed in any detail Messrs Stone and Swain initiated a system of community consultation. Together with officers from County Hall they elicited from individuals and organisations in the town what in fact they wanted, thus ensuring from the outset an important degree of co-operation and community involvement. Another feature of Sutton Centre has been its situation, planted right in the middle of town, easily accessible to shoppers, shopkeepers and office workers with the result that it keeps the town centre alive after normal working hours.

Contiguity seems to have played a part also in inducing Derbyshire to develop its own system of community education. Although it was early in the field, Hope Valley College being opened by Morris himself in 1959, the idea became dormant for many years; today, however, the authority is once more beginning to encourage the development of its schools as community colleges. The same process is noticeable in Devon, where early moves were made to establish community schools. These were impelled by the Chief Education Officer, Elmslie Phillip, who had worked with Morris in Shire Hall, as an assistant, before the war. In the development plan which he presented to his committee in 1945 he wrote: 'In years to come we shall find ourselves thinking more in terms of social, educational and recreational centres, whether in towns or villages, of which one part is devoted to the education of children during some of the daytime.' Quiescent for some years after Phillip's retirement, today Devon schools are actively seeking ways to involve the surrounding community in self-directed study and recreation.

In Cheshire special attention has been given to developing primary schools as places where the local community is able to find a centre for their meetings and for courses. And in Crewe the Cheshire County Council was helped with a large new community school by the D.E.S., whose well-disposed Architects and Buildings branch designed the building for them. The big cities have developed community education in various different ways.

London had been slow to move but already three big comprehensives have been designated as community schools and are going ahead to provide opportunities for adults not merely to use the premises for traditional adult classes, which has always been a feature of London education, but for courses where they in fact find themselves sitting with and working with school students and where school facilities are made available to the community. At the same time, certain London schools, in co-operation with the university Institute of Education, are working on the development of a community curriculum, a field of whose importance Morris was well aware (see page 75), which has been explored and developed in many parts of the country, but which is hampered not a little by our attachment to a rigid system of public examinations.

Local government has not been made entirely impotent by successive attempts by Whitehall, or by the attempts of successive governments, to take it over. Community education has remained an area where the decision as to whether or not an L.E.A. 'goes community' is still left to local councillors, strongly influenced by the prejudices or predilections of their chief education officers. Progress has been slower than Morris hoped for, slower indeed than he expected, but it can already be seen that step by step, county by county and city by city community education is spreading over the whole country.

Already the Community Education Association, founded in 1979 and with a fast-growing membership, has spread nationwide. Its regional organisation, started in 1983, means that members everywhere have local contacts and can organise meetings in their area. It also ensures that the executive committee of the association is drawn from a wide geographical area. Membership is open to professionals and others, to those working inside and outside the school system, to administrators, governors, politicians and parents. In areas where community education is still ignored, members press for it to be established; in areas where it is established they press for its extension and development. The annual conference of C.E.A. attracts guests of national reputation and enthusiastic participators, while the membership is kept in touch through the C.E.D.C.'s monthly publication.

'Each age is a dream that is dying, and one that is coming to birth.' It was with this quotation from Shelley that Henry Morris opened his address to the British Association at Blackpool in 1936. The dying dream of a state system of schooling geared to eliminate the majority from education before they have come out of their teens is giving way to Morris's dream of a state system where 'We have raised the school leaving age to 90.' 'Where every single being is significated in the economic and cultural order'...'where every local community becomes an educational society, and where education becomes not merely a consequence of good government, but good government a consequence of education.'

Selection of reports and works referred to

Association of Directors and Secretaries for Education, *Post-War Policy* (' *The Orange Book*') HMSO, 1942 (page 55)

This was the relatively minor outcome of a potentially important initiative taken by wartime Chief Education Officers. They decided to produce a full statement of educational aims for the post-war period. The resulting 'book' was a slim, cheaply produced pamphlet, highly platitudinous and pompous. The best thing to emerge from it were the papers written by Henry Morris (reproduced here) which he submitted to his colleagues for consideration when the book was first mooted. They were ignored at the time.

Board of Education, *Handbook of Suggestions for Teachers*, HMSO, 1937 (page 66)

A document produced by H.M.I. in which highly educated subject specialists working at a great distance from the majority of classrooms, attempted to indicate how their culture could be conveyed to the masses by teachers.

Consultative Committee of the Board of Education, *The Education of the Adolescent* (Hadow Report) HMSO, 1926 (page 11)

The Consultative Committee of the Board of Education was a standing committee, composed mainly of academics, which was expected to produce advice for the President of the Board (i.e. Minister of Education) on future education policy. When Lord Hadow was chairman his report started the re-organisation of elementary schools, splitting them up into separate schools by age into Junior (5–11) and Senior (11–15).

Morris, H. '*Amusement and Education*'. Paper to All Souls Group, October 1953 (page 9)

Originally this Group, which met first early in the Second World War at the invitation of W. G. S. Adams, Warden of All Souls, in the college, was set up to include mainly Chief Education Officers but was quickly extended to civil servants, M.P.s, H.M.I.s etc. They never met again in All Souls, but they have clung to the label. Morris took a delight in writing a paper for the Group in which he castigated the low level of popular entertainment and culture.

Morris, H. *Report on the West African Institute of Industries, Arts and Social Science*, Colonial Office, November 1947 (pages 8 and 9)

A report written by Morris after his visit to Accra in 1947, and submitted after a year's delay, to the Colonial Office, who had initiated the visit.

Rée, H. *Educator Extraordinary, The Life and Achievement of Henry Morris*, Longman, 1973 (page 10)

This full biography of Morris attempts to show the close but not obvious link between Morris's personal and public life and describes the achievement of Morris during a rather arid period of educational history.